PROBLEM MANAG

CW01508132

BCS, THE CHARTERED INSTITUTE FOR IT

BCS, The Chartered Institute for IT champions the global IT profession and the interests of individuals engaged in that profession for the benefit of all. We promote wider social and economic progress through the advancement of information technology, science and practice. We bring together industry, academics, practitioners and government to share knowledge, promote new thinking, inform the design of new curricula, shape public policy and inform the public.

Our vision is to be a world-class organisation for IT. Our 70,000 strong membership includes practitioners, businesses, academics and students in the UK and internationally. We deliver a range of professional development tools for practitioners and employees. A leading IT qualification body, we offer a range of widely recognised qualifications.

Further Information
BCS, The Chartered Institute for IT,
First Floor, Block D,
North Star House, North Star Avenue,
Swindon, SN2 1FA, United Kingdom.
T +44 (0) 1793 417 424
F +44 (0) 1793 417 444
www.bcs.org/contact

http://shop.bcs.org/

PROBLEM MANAGEMENT
An implementation guide for the real world

Michael G. Hall

© 2014 Michael G. Hall

All rights reserved. Apart from any fair dealing for the purposes of research or private study, or criticism or review, as permitted by the Copyright Designs and Patents Act 1988, no part of this publication may be reproduced, stored or transmitted in any form or by any means, except with the prior permission in writing of the publisher, or in the case of reprographic reproduction, in accordance with the terms of the licences issued by the Copyright Licensing Agency. Enquiries for permission to reproduce material outside those terms should be directed to the publisher.

All trade marks, registered names etc. acknowledged in this publication are the property of their respective owners. BCS and the BCS logo are the registered trade marks of the British Computer Society charity number 292786 (BCS).

ITIL® and IT Infrastructure Library® are Registered Trademarks of AXELOS in the United Kingdom and other countries.

Published by BCS Learning & Development Ltd, a wholly owned subsidiary of BCS, The Chartered Institute for IT, First Floor, Block D, North Star House, North Star Avenue, Swindon, SN2 1FA, UK.
www.bcs.org

ISBN: 978-1-78017-241-5
PDF ISBN: 978-1-78017-242-2
ePUB ISBN: 978-1-78017-243-9
Kindle ISBN: 978-1-78017-244-6

British Cataloguing in Publication Data.
A CIP catalogue record for this book is available at the British Library.

Disclaimer:
The views expressed in this book are of the author(s) and do not necessarily reflect the views of the Institute or BCS Learning & Development Ltd except where explicitly stated as such. Although every care has been taken by the author(s) and BCS Learning & Development Ltd in the preparation of the publication, no warranty is given by the author(s) or BCS Learning & Development Ltd as publisher as to the accuracy or completeness of the information contained within it and neither the author(s) nor BCS Learning & Development Ltd shall be responsible or liable for any loss or damage whatsoever arising by virtue of such information or any instructions or advice contained within this publication or by any of the aforementioned.

BCS books are available at special quantity discounts to use as premiums and sale promotions, or for use in corporate training programmes. Please visit our Contact us page at www.bcs.org/contact

Typeset by Lapiz Digital Services, Chennai, India.

CONTENTS

FIGURES AND TABLES

AUTHOR

Michael has over 25 years' experience in IT, developing and leading teams, managing change programmes and implementing service management. Now a specialist in service operations, he founded problem management as a global function at Deutsche Bank. He is a Chartered IT Professional (CITP).

He has been a regular presenter on service management topics for ITSMF UK – including at the annual conference in November 2012 – and is now active in Australia. He has been contributing to a series of white papers on service management, and several more are in preparation.

In 2012, he earned a Masters degree in Business and Technology from the Australian Graduate School of Management, and in 2013 returned to Australia following several years in the UK.

ACKNOWLEDGEMENTS

I am indebted to Joe Gallagher, my former colleague at Deutsche Bank Problem Management, for some lively discussion of and deeply thoughtful contribution to the practice of problem management. I have drawn on his experiences in implementing and running problem management at several organisations, but in particular in our time together at Deutsche Bank, where the problem management function was considered by many to be a highly developed and effective implementation.

To Dennis Adams, of Dennis Adams Associates in the UK, I am grateful for permission to use his ideas about the problem advisory board, a great approach that should be more widely adopted. Thanks also to Chris Finden-Browne, previously with IBM for many years and now gracefully retired, who helped me early on by debating the concepts important to problem management, as well as for the original of a diagram about incident and problem management, which I have drawn on in this book. To David Ireland and James Bourgerie, who gave me the trigger to start writing, something I had been intending to do for while, when they came to me with their book, already well advanced.

I acknowledge colleagues in problem management from other organisations, met through organisations such as ITSMF, including Barry Corless from Global Knowledge, the BCS Service Management Special Interest Group, the many LinkedIn™ problem management blogs, Paul Soutar, Stuart Kendricks, Paul Offord from Advance 7, and many more.

I would also like to thank all the authors of the many books on service management, problem-solving, human error, system failure, system and data analysis and process management that I have drawn on for quotes and guidance. These are listed in the references and under further reading.

I owe a special debt to Jutta Mackwell of BCS, who has led me through the process of getting this book from an idea to the finished article. Her patience with me as a new author and especially her enormous attention to detail in editing and correcting my abysmal grammar have made it all possible. It could not have happened without her.

Finally, I would like to make a special acknowledgement to Dan Skwire, author of *First Fault Software Problem Solving*, for his advice and encouragement to keep going, finish and publish.

INTRODUCTION

This book started from a question by a colleague on LinkedIn™, asking if anyone could recommend any books on implementing problem management. At the time, we found that there were many books out there on the process and, in particular, on techniques for and approaches to root cause analysis or problem-solving itself, but nothing on how to get problem management started.

WHAT THIS BOOK IS ABOUT

This book is specifically about implementing and then running a successful and effective problem management function. It is based on real-world experiences in implementing problem management in large and small organisations. It also looks at the organisational issues of running problem management, such as stakeholder management, to realise real value for the organisation. In other words, it is about handling problems in volume as opposed to solving individual problems.

The book aims to fill the gap between theoretical knowledge (perhaps obtained by studying and sitting exams for ITIL® Foundation or Expert) and turning that knowledge into an effective operation. The practical guidance, templates, advice and suggestions included in this book are intended to be used and tailored to your situation.

To cater to as wide an audience as possible, the book does not assume any more knowledge of problem management than is mentioned in ITIL. Having said that, if you are unfamiliar with ITIL, don't be too concerned, because everything I cover is either self-evident or explained in the book. For those with extensive problem management knowledge, I offer apologies in advance for places where I spell out what seems obvious. However, very little in this book is going over ground already comprehensively covered in the ITIL publications.

WHAT THIS BOOK IS NOT ABOUT

Although summarised in Section 3, this book is not about detailed problem-solving techniques. There are so many very good books already out there, it seemed to be less useful to go back over this area. However, the importance of structure in problem-solving, as well as a detailed look at the overall process, are covered comprehensively, along with some thoughts and suggestions about how to get this right and how to win people over to adopting a consistent and structured approach.

WHY READ THIS BOOK?

The primary audience for this book is people who are involved in IT support in some way. You are most probably involved in a service-oriented production support organisation and very likely one that is considering or has used ITIL as a basic organising principle.

If you are in that situation, several issues might be driving you to look for a book about problem management:

- You see the need and want to convince management and the rest of your organisation that problem management is worth doing.
- You have been asked to implement problem management and you are looking for some guidance.
- You already have a problem management function, but it isn't very effective or realising the benefits expected. Your objective is to turn the situation around and make problem management as effective as you think it can be.
- You already have a problem management function that is effective. You just want to see what other ideas are out there that you could pick up to help lift your organisation's problem management to the next level.

At this point, it is important to note that problem management is not just for IT. There is a wide application to operations and business practices and processes of all types. There is definitely a crossover in the literature on root cause analysis from the quality assurance, human factors and system safety disciplines, as well as with process improvement techniques, such as Lean and Six Sigma. Problem management is a discipline with wide application.

BIASES

Like all authors, I have my own opinions and biases. As an implementer and practitioner of problem management, I have found that some things work better than others and I tend to favour those approaches. If you have found to the contrary in your travels, please understand and forgive my point of view.

As far as possible, I have tried to avoid an 'it depends' mentality. Recommendations are firm and opinionated, leaving it up to you to decide whether they are right or relevant for your situation.

SECTIONS

This book is organised into three sections.

Section 1 'Introducing problem management'

To help you understand why problem management will benefit your organisation, this section first summarises what problem management is and what it aims to achieve.

It explains how problem management differs from incident management, then goes on to discuss key factors to consider for a proposal. A detailed discussion of how to develop a business case for problem management then follows, including topics such as the benefits case, return on investment, estimating the business costs of service interruption, a summary of implementation costs to consider and measuring the actual benefits obtained. Section 1 concludes with what to include in a high-level implementation project plan.

Section 2 'Implementation and running problem management'

We now get into the details of the implementation. After discussing the organisational change factors that need to be considered and managed, this section delves into the implementation approach and phasing. Next, it discusses organising as a function, covering the people and skills that are needed, the training required, the different models or structures that can be employed, various governance considerations and problem management in outsourced environments. A chapter on realising the benefits covers essential factors needed to ensure success, followed by one on key performance indicators, metrics and reporting and tool selection requirements. Section 2 ends with some thoughts on where problem management might be going and how it could be applied in other areas and business functions.

Section 3 'Problem management process and techniques'

This section deals with the process and techniques. It is intended as a reference manual rather than something that needs to be read in one sitting and is structured around a step-through of the process, focusing on the important factors to get right as well as highlighting a few areas where I feel the ITIL approach could be improved. The chapter on investigation and diagnosis summarises all the major and minor techniques for problem-solving, with references to relevant books and articles for those who want further information.

Online resources

An online resources section covers sample business cases, a sample implementation plan, a set of recommended root cause codes and a listing of useful books related to problem management.

CONVENTIONS USED IN THIS BOOK

Masked examples

Quite a few of the examples used in this book are drawn from frank conversations with colleagues in the USA, the UK and Australia. Although there are no trade secrets on view, many felt that they did not want to publicise problems and other data that might reflect negatively on their organisations, so I have generally not named organisations.

Symbols

A definition, whether from ITIL, my own or from elsewhere.

Things to think about or consider as options, perhaps a little bit 'out of the box'.

Shortcuts to success and approaches I have found to work well.

A recommendation, something that I think is mandatory for success.

Cross-references

You will probably not read this book like a novel, from start to finish. Topics are cross-referenced to allow you to track back and forwards, or to catch up on topics that you might have skipped.

SECTION 1 – INTRODUCING PROBLEM MANAGEMENT

The title has a deliberate double meaning and the chapters included in this section have two separate but related aims:

- Firstly, to introduce problem management to you and confirm your understanding of what it is and what it does, so that you can persuasively explain it to others.

- Secondly, to outline a practical business case for introducing problem management into your organisation or area.

Of course, how you build or modify the business case depends on your particular situation and organisation. For example:

- There might be a lack of transparency. Customers and management are worried about their risk exposure to incidents that have affected them. They don't know what is going on, whether problems are being investigated or being fixed, or whether and when an incident will recur, with more impact on their business processes.

- There might be a concern about the lack of effective problem-solving techniques. Support teams are not equipped with the skills and tools to solve the problems they face; there is a lot of variation in the skill levels of staff; and no well-understood, consistent and repeatable process is in place to manage problems as they arise.

- The stability of the IT services offered might be poor or even getting worse. If it is improving, it is not doing so quickly enough to satisfy management, customers or the IT service teams themselves.

- Root cause investigation might be working well; however, it might be challenging to get the fixes implemented that are needed to resolve the causes.

- Outsourced, vendor-managed or cloud-sourced service delivery models make it difficult to resolve problems.

- Or all of the above in some combination.

It is important to know from where you are starting. A careful assessment will help you decide what the most important issues are and what needs to be addressed first. This is covered in Chapter 2, as well as in Chapter 5.

1 WHAT IS PROBLEM MANAGEMENT?

So what is problem management and what does it aim to achieve? And how is it different from incident management?

OBJECTIVES

This is what *ITIL Service Operation* (Cabinet Office, 2011, page 97) says problem management is all about:

- Prevent problems and resulting incidents from happening.
- Eliminate recurring incidents.
- Minimise the impact of incidents that cannot be prevented.

In other words, problem management is about improving stability across platforms. There is quite a lot of excellent guidance in the problem management section of the 2011 edition of the *ITIL Service Operation* book. The chapter is only about 14 pages long and well worth reading in detail. The following short section draws on some of this material, as well as on practical experience and other sources.

SCOPE

ITIL distinguishes between reactive and proactive problem management. This is a debatable distinction because the only real difference between the two types of problem activities is in how the problem is detected. It causes extensive discussion in the problem management community of practice. See Chapter 11 for more on this topic.

Reactive problem management is where the problem management process flows from an incident that has occurred (Figure 1.1 – I am indebted to Chris Finden-Browne, a Distinguished Engineer at IBM UK, who produced the original version of this diagram).

Once service has been restored, at least partially, problem management follows on from incident management to investigate the root cause and implement a fix to prevent the incident happening again.

Proactive problem management is where the emphasis is on identifying and resolving problems **before** they cause incidents (Figure 1.2).

Figure 1.1 Reactive problem management

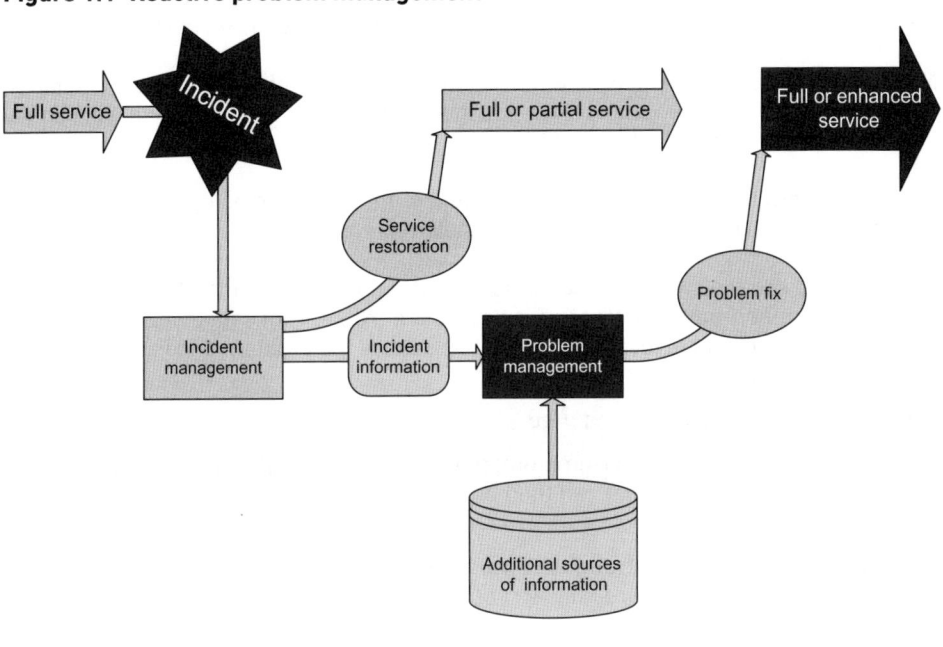

Figure 1.2 Proactive problem management

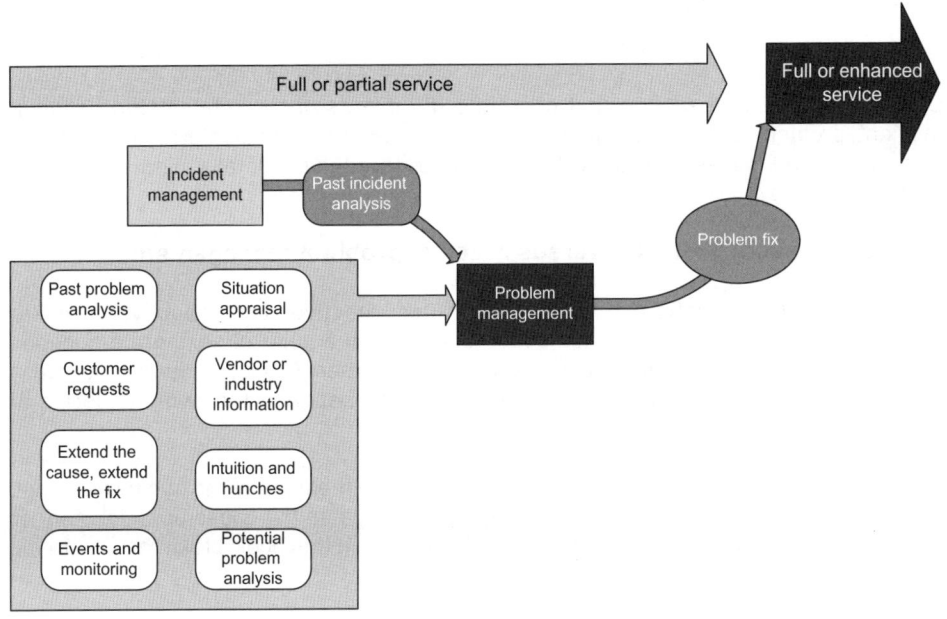

Proactive problem management uses data such as patterns and trends, monitoring, knowledge, the outputs of other processes and intuition to find potential problems. Chapter 11 provides in-depth coverage of how this analysis can be approached.

Naturally, it is better to find a problem and fix it proactively before it causes an incident; however, this is not always possible, so effective investigation and correction will usually be required after an incident as well.

Once a problem has been identified ('detected' in the ITIL terminology), the process is the same for both reactive and proactive problems:

- Diagnose the real cause of the actual or potential problem. Effective problem management requires methods for finding the true or root cause and showing 'beyond a reasonable level of doubt' that it causes the problem and is not just a symptom or an apparent cause.

- Determine the resolution required.

- Ensure that the resolution is implemented completely. That is, a fix needs to be developed and applied that can then be tested in some way to prove that it has eliminated the problem.

- Maintain information, throughout the problem life cycle, in a format that is useful for the future and readily accessible, including:
  - the root cause;
  - any workarounds that were used to recover from further incidents while the fix was being developed and applied;
  - the resolution that was implemented;
  - any lessons learned and so on.

Chapter 6 contains a section that goes into the details of the relationship between incident, problem and knowledge management and how the known error records this information and makes it available. Section 3 goes through the details of how to achieve these objectives.

The debate about proactive versus reactive problem management

Surprisingly, the question of what constitutes reactive and proactive problem management is the subject of much debate, even to the point of asking the question 'Is there any such thing as proactive problem management?' The *ITIL Service Operation* book (Cabinet Office, 2011, pp.97–99) differentiates between the two categories of problems, but it is not very definitive.

The labels themselves are useful, but debate about the meaning of the two terms is not. It does not matter whether a problem directly investigates the cause of an incident or incidents or if it is found in some other way. Therefore, in this book, I take the pragmatic approach as follows:

There is more to problem management than just reacting to incidents as they occur. It is more effective to look at the many other ways that possible problems in the environment can be discovered and try to do something about them before they cause incidents.

PROBLEM MANAGEMENT IS DIFFERENT FROM INCIDENT MANAGEMENT

When introducing problem management, the difference between it and incident management can often be the most difficult concept to get across to staff and management. Getting people to understand that incident and problem management have different objectives and benefits is a critical success factor for any implementation.

Although incident and problem management aim to achieve very different outcomes, the words 'incident', 'problem', 'outage' and similar terms are often used interchangeably by customers, as well as by IT staff. It makes sense to distinguish between an incident – a full or partial failure to a service being used by a customer – and a problem – the underlying cause of an incident, which must be found and eliminated to prevent more occurrences of that incident. ITIL introduced the two terms 'incident' and 'problem' to make this distinction. The aims of incident management and problem management are different.

- **Incident management** has a primary focus on restoring service rapidly to minimise the down time and business impact of incidents. It is justifiably reactive by nature and does not (or should not) focus on underlying causes. Although excellent incident management can reduce business impact by reducing down time, by itself it cannot reduce the number of service interruptions in the long term, because it does not focus on finding causes and eliminating them. The emphasis is very firmly on **what** is wrong and putting it right, not on **why** it happened – it is about finding the immediate cause of the service interruption and removing it, so that services start working again. This immediate cause can also be referred to as the indicative, proximate or technical cause. Finding the root cause (why the immediate cause happened) is not the objective, although it is at times required to restore service.

- **Problem management** investigates to find the **real** cause, usually referred to as the root cause. Once the cause is established, problem management then makes sure that the problem is fixed **completely**, so that it cannot happen again. To reiterate, the aim is to:
  - establish the real reason for either an incident that has occurred, or a risk or situation that has potential to cause an incident; and then to
  - execute a plan to fix the cause permanently.

An example of how the approaches differ is a recent episode where I had a strange printer issue. For an unknown reason, the print dialogue box looked different from usual and printing did not work. The service desk referred the incident to the desktop support team, who solved the incident by deleting all the installed printers from the laptop and adding them back, which forced them to pick up freshly installed printer drivers from the server. This resolved the incident and printing now worked. At this point, it was job done, case closed.

Although it was an example of good incident management, it was an unsatisfying experience from a problem manager's point of view. Questions such as why it happened, whether it would happen again and if others were affected were all left unanswered.

Incident and problem management are complementary and work closely together to achieve the desired outcome of reducing the number and impact of incidents. Incident management reduces impact by applying a structured and organised approach to restoring service as quickly as possible. The objective is to minimise the business impact of an incident that has actually happened. Problem management reduces the overall number of incidents through finding and fixing problems before they cause future incidents, as well as stopping repeat incidents by fixing problems after they have triggered incidents.

In practice, incident management should hand off smoothly to problem management at some point. Unfortunately, it is common for the line between the two to blur – it is not always clear when incident management stops and problem management starts. In fact, the relationship between incident management and problem management is one of the most important to discuss, make clear and formalise as part of the problem management implementation project. The best organisations put a lot of effort into getting this right and I discuss how best to achieve it in Chapter 11.

Now that we have clarified what problem management is about, let us move on to look at some of the factors that are critical to a successful implementation.

2 FACTORS FOR SUCCESS

Personal experience has shown that several factors make the difference between a good implementation and a less successful one. I want to highlight:

- some common challenges every implementation faces;
- winning the support of management;
- the importance of training;
- stakeholder management and communications; and
- the decisions and agreements that need to be made before you can propose the implementation of problem management.

CHALLENGES

Starting point

It might sound obvious to say this, but it is important to know where you are starting from, so that you know how big a change implementing problem management is going to be. As mentioned in the introduction to this section, different organisations will have different priorities, attitudes and 'maturity'. Comparing perception with reality can be revealing, particularly if there are measurements available to define the current state. An obvious measurement is the number of incidents and their impact, duration and whether the numbers are constant or trending up or down. What does this measure say about stability and the quality of the current IT service? That is, is the situation getting better or worse, or staying the same? What about the number of recurring incidents (incidents that have the same or similar underlying causes, or are perceived to be the same or of the same type)? In addition, are there any unresolved problems in the environment (perceived or real), and if so, how many?

Assessing the starting point should be evidence-based as far as possible; however, a survey of opinions is also a good tool. Asking questions of both the IT community and its clients and customers can assist in estimating where you are starting from. Note the use of the inclusive 'we' in the following examples, rather than the outsider's 'you':

- Are we good at solving problems? (You might get some surprising answers to this one, depending on people's perceptions of what this phrase means.)
- Do problems persist for a long time in the environment?

- If we could improve one thing about problem management, what would it be?
- Are incidents resolved and don't happen again, or do incidents tend to repeat?
- What concerns or issues do we see that impact our business operations?

It is important to realise that some form of problem management is already taking place in every organisation. It might not be recognised as such, it might not be very effective, but it is definitely happening. Therefore, the starting point is never zero and the implementation is always an improvement initiative (England, 2011, p.7).

Gather information at many levels, including talking to different management and staff levels among the business customers of IT (if that is possible). Some example questions might be:

- How do you rate the stability of IT systems?
- What improvements would you like to see?
- What systems or processes give you the most concern?
- How hard is it to change the way things are done?
- What do you see as the biggest obstacle to making improvements?

As always when talking to people about IT, it pays to be wary of the responses, as people's opinions might be biased or coloured by a recent unsatisfactory occurrence. Take care to assess the context of responses. If nothing else, survey results and answers to questions will highlight some problems in the environment that might feed into quick wins for the implementation.

A framework for assessing maturity such as COBIT® is a useful way of understanding where you are starting from as well. The COBIT® model assesses maturity on a six point scale from zero (non-existent) to five (optimised) in areas such as:

- awareness and communications;
- policies, plans and procedures;
- tools and automation;
- skills and expertise;
- responsibility and accountability;
- goal setting and measurement.

(Dugmore and Lacy, 2011, p.39)

There are many online resources available to help you assess maturity. Two examples are the *CMMI Appraisals* from the CMMI Institute (CMMI, 2014) and the *COBIT® Self-Assessment Guide* from ISACA (ISACA, 2013).

The size of the change required is affected by the starting point. Assess issues such as whether a separate production support function exists, how good the interaction is within and between teams and whether people in different roles (such as infrastructure support, application support and development) are used to working together or tend to operate in silos. Based on the quality of these interactions, decide where your organisation is on the spectrum.

Current attitudes

Some of your colleagues might not want to engage in problem management. There are many reasons for this:

- Not everyone wants problems solved. We have probably all seen the hero-mode technical support specialist or incident manager, who might be challenged by the idea of doing away with operating in crisis mode. They might feel it is the justification for their role. These people might feel that fixing problems could make them unnecessary. Compare firefighters with fire prevention officers: the former sounds like more fun than the latter. Besides, what do firefighters do with themselves when there aren't any fires to fight?

- It might be that certain people might not want the causes of problems to be revealed. They might have concerns about exposing their lack of competence, or having management discover that rewards they have received were unjustified. Perhaps they received praise for a project delivered on time and budget, when in reality there were inherent faults in what they designed or delivered. I have personal experience of an application that was old and not well documented. Nobody really knew exactly how it worked anymore, so the cause of any failure tended to be deflected onto other things ('latency', for instance) to hide the fact that it was an unsupportable application. This had become the status quo over several years. While this is an extreme case, it is not as rare as you might think.

- Trust might be an issue, particularly if people have suffered from a blame culture in their current or previous organisations. In these situations, there might be a suspicion that the problem management process will be used to 'find the culprits', point fingers or hand out punishments. The only way around this is to emphasise that problem management is focused on the cause of the problem, not 'who did it'. A strong assertion that problem management will not assign blame, backed up by performance that demonstrates this approach, has been shown to be one way to win the confidence of stakeholders.

- Very commonly, there is an embedded culture, particularly in fast-paced organisations such as finance, to report 'root cause' very rapidly, well before a reasonable investigation could possibly have taken place. They will feel that problem management is too slow for them and will not meet their requirements for speed. It is very hard to shift this behaviour. A method for dealing with this is set out under 'Effective communication' in Chapter 6.

- Simple inertia can also be a barrier. Unless people understand and get behind the idea that there is a better way to do things, there will be no incentive to move away from the status quo.

All of these issues might actively undermine your problem management initiative. Section 2 suggests some methods that I have used successfully to deal with these situations.

Organisational behavioural change

Implementing problem management is, of itself, an organisational change initiative and, as experts going as far back as Niccolò Machiavelli have noted, getting people to change how they do things is the hardest of all activities:

> One should bear in mind that there is nothing more difficult to execute, nor more dubious of success, nor more dangerous to administer, than to introduce new political orders. For the one who introduces them has as his enemies all those who profit from the old order, and he has only lukewarm defenders in all those who might profit from the new order. This lukewarmness ... arises ... partly from the incredulity of men, who do not truly believe in new things unless they have actually had personal experience of them. (Machiavelli, 1513, p.22)

There is no getting around the fact that the introduction of problem management requires a change of behaviour, at least for some people or at least to some degree. Logic does not necessarily work in changing attitudes, and careful attention to how to work through the change process is needed to avoid failure. A good, practical and mercifully short guide to understanding how change works is *How to save time and money by managing organisational change effectively* (Gilbert and Hutchinson, 2009).

Changing attitudes and work practices is relevant in several places in the process:

- adopting problem management in the first place;
- handing over incidents properly to problem management;
- doing root cause analysis in a structured way;
- implementing solutions to resolve problems.

All these are covered in detail in later chapters. In addition, both the business case and implementation plan need to address them specifically in order to start the awareness process, and to plan and manage the change of attitude required.

Introducing problem management into an organisation is the type of change that requires people to actually do it before it becomes part of the way they do things: 'Seeing trumps hearing, but doing trumps seeing' (Vietnamese proverb quoted in Pascale, Sternin and Sternin, 2010, p.34). Rather than just telling people about the process, particularly the problem-solving techniques that should be introduced, the implementation will be more successful if it gets people actually practising and therefore learning by doing.

To get the best results from implementing problem management, it is important to gain commitment to the programme, not just compliance with a set of rules leading to minimal long-term effects. The more people take up the process and see the benefits, the more committed they will become.

Of course, there are some people who might never accept or adopt change, no matter what the situation. This attitude has nothing to do with problem management itself, it is simply that, while almost everyone finds change difficult to some degree, some individuals cannot deal with change very well at all.

Cost

Some people might not initially understand the difference between incident management and problem management, so the latter can look like an additional cost and resource burden on top of what is already being done. In reality, problem management is self-funding, provided you can show results in terms of reducing the negative business impact of incidents, which implies of course that the cost of down time needs to be known. Experience shows that through improved stability and reduced adverse business impact from interruptions to key processes, the returns from problem management easily cover the costs of the resources, training and systems involved in its implementation. We consider how to quantify this return on investment in Chapter 3.

Business needs convincing

Convincing your business customers (or even their customers) of the merits of problem management is probably less of an issue than might be expected. Firstly, problem management will not necessarily be visible to them, because it tends to happen within the service organisation. Secondly, they are probably suffering from service interruptions anyway and will readily accept a proposal to do something about the source of the pain. In reality, handled properly they could be useful allies to enlist in winning IT management support for the implementation.

Terminology

One of the strengths of ITIL® is the consistent terminology it provides to service organisations. Using the defined terms properly makes communication clearer and reinforces understanding. Having said that, in fact ITIL® has a few terms that might need careful explanation – 'problem', 'workaround', 'known error' – as well as a few that do not have definitions, such as 'problems without a workaround'.

Customers will almost certainly find the terminology confusing. When you hear 'Houston, we have a problem', you probably know what is meant. It is unlikely that the reaction would be 'Sorry Apollo, don't you mean incident?' You could educate your customers in correct terminology, or simply accept the fact that they will use words that make sense to them, while educating your internal staff to know the difference and cope with the external world in suitable terms. If the word 'problem' is not well understood, you might find you have to talk to your customers about the 'underlying causes of incidents' until the terms become embedded. Several organisations report that often customers tend to become the ones pushing the correct terms even when IT staff are reluctant to change.

It is worth making the effort to include both the definition of terms in any training you provide and then go on to use the terms consistently. Also remember that, as you recruit staff, either they will bring an understanding of the standard ITIL® terms with them, or you will have to make sure that they quickly acquire this knowledge.

None of these six challenges is insurmountable. In fact, as good problem managers should do, defining the problem is the first part of solving it, so once these factors are understood, solutions can be discussed, agreed and built into the business case and the plan.

MANAGEMENT SUPPORT

Implementing problem management without management support and buy-in is possible, just much more difficult than it needs to be. If you are fortunate, your IT organisation has embraced ITIL® or a similar framework, and is aligned to a service-oriented culture. When management understands the required functions, introducing problem management will be part of the overall implementation or, if already implemented, it will be a case of improving the problem management function. Focus on selling the concept, the structure and the benefits to confirm support, set expectations and clear up any misconceptions. If you are not in this position, you need to be more careful with the justification for problem management, covered in detail in Chapter 3. Along with stakeholder management, winning management support is probably one of the most critical success factors. Leverage it if you have it, or if you do not, win it through effective communication.

TRAINING

Training has been shown to be a significant success factor in addressing the factors I mentioned earlier, such as the lack of awareness of what problem management is, what it does and the distinction between incident management and problem management. This training includes both specialised training for people identified to become (or continue to be) problem managers and incident managers, and familiarisation training for the general technical and business support community, as well as for management, especially senior management if possible. Both help to set expectations correctly about what problem management is, what it aims to achieve, how the process is conducted and what outcomes to expect and when.

It is therefore important to design, build and deliver training about problem management as part of any implementation or re-launch project. The training can be done in-house and doesn't have to be expensive, apart from people's time, and the cost will be well worth it for the benefit gained. A suggested familiarisation training course is included in Chapter 5.

STAKEHOLDER MANAGEMENT

> Stakeholders are those people who have a vested interest in your project, whether they want it to succeed or fail. Winning over the people who fall into the latter category will really make it easier to run the project. One of the ways to do that is to establish what they want from the project and find a way to give it to them. (Harrin, 2007, p.119)

This definition is from a book on project management, but substitute 'problem management' for 'your project' and the sense is entirely appropriate. Successful implementation of problem management depends upon identifying both the positive and negative attitudes of stakeholders and addressing each of them, not only in the proposal, but also in the implementation planning phase. Stakeholder management is all about understanding the motivations of each stakeholder or group, their wants, desires, and political position and alliances. Map them into a simple-to-understand diagram or table, and then develop individual plans for each.

Taking time to understand each stakeholder group's concerns helps position where the importance of problem management sits for them – high or low, central or peripheral. Do not assume anything, but make sure that you talk to your stakeholders or work with someone who can.

For example, what are the drivers for the IT management team? Apart from the ever-present focus on costs, they might be concerned about stability and reducing down time, or buying or building a new data centre. Management will also be thinking strategically about new developments in response to business demands, such as a major deployment supporting a significant business initiative, dealing with a merger or acquisition, or introducing business process automation. They might even be in the middle of outsourcing or insourcing services.

Planning and communication strategies will then flow from this understanding, reducing the chances of mis-selling the initiative and improving your chances of success. The stakeholder management plan is covered in Chapter 4.

COMMUNICATION

Effective communication is the tool needed to overcome the inertia that inhibits change (see 'Challenges' earlier). People need to know not only what problem management is and why it being implemented, but also what's in it for them. This is why planning the communications part of the implementation is so important. Right from the initial pitch to management to win support, everything should be coordinated to maximise the awareness of the benefits to all your stakeholders. Apart from the trust challenge mentioned earlier, which needs to be overcome through direct experience of how problem management works, each of the challenges highlighted can be at least partly addressed through sharing information. It is important to talk about, and then get agreement for, what will be communicated, how and when. This becomes the communication plan, which, like the stakeholder management plan, is a critical part of the implementation.

The initial communications should focus on answering 'what's in it for me?' for each stakeholder group. The message can then be reinforced in the familiarisation training materials, especially for the key technical expert groups that need to get involved directly in the problem management process. You can build on the familiarisation training by reporting regularly on your key performance indicators (KPIs – see Chapter 7) and especially by reporting successes in implementing permanent fixes to long-standing problems. It can feel unnatural for IT service and support teams to communicate in this way. It is quite common to assume that everyone knows what you are achieving, but that is far from the truth. So, as well as reporting progress in your implementation project, don't be afraid to identify and target the low hanging fruit.

Once established, reporting on progress and achievements then becomes part of the routine running of the problem management function, addressing the related issues of managing risk perceptions and the lack of transparency, as well as managing the overall incident to problem life cycle covered in Section 3. An effective communication model is mapped out in Chapter 6.

CONSISTENT APPROACH

A consistent method for problem-solving is a key requirement for effective problem management. If everyone has a standardised set of skills and all talk the same language, life is much simpler. The basic ingredient of success is to come up with one structured, evidence-based approach and allow it to evolve as the process matures. One organisation I am familiar with found that, by implementing structured problem-solving (Kepner–Tregoe in their case), they were able to reduce the time to find root cause from about 10 days on average to three days, a 60 per cent improvement.

There are as many methods as there are books about problem-solving; however, the similarities are generally greater than the differences. The *ITIL Service Operation* book gives an overview of some (Cabinet Office, 2011, pp.99–101) and I list some more good books on the subject in the Further reading section. In addition, a comprehensive discussion of most of the major approaches to root cause analysis can be found in Chapter 13.

Consistency is important for all organisation types, but in a larger organisation, where there might be several problem managers in operation, it is even more so. With different problem managers running their investigations using methods and approaches to suit themselves, the subject matter experts (SMEs) who are engaged with them in root cause analysis are going to be presented with a range of different approaches and styles. It can be quite confusing, will affect the credibility of the process and is likely to lead to inconsistent results. It would be much better if an agreed, standard and consistent approach was in use, with all investigation sessions following a set agenda with predictable and agreed deliverables.

People generally like consistency and structure, and knowing what to expect. After a while it becomes second nature, part of 'the way we do things around here' and drops from conscious view. At that point, the organisational culture will have been changed successfully.

Related to this issue is paying attention to the selection, aptitude and skills of your problem managers. Whether you use dedicated, fully trained problem managers or people who do problem management part-time as part of their other roles, these individuals must have the skills and aptitude, backed up by the right training in a structured approach to problem resolution, to be truly effective at finding causes and driving the implementation of fixes. Nothing has proved to be more effective in implementing problem management than improving the skills of new and existing problem managers and taking extra care in the recruitment process.

AGREEMENTS

Quite a few agreements need to be reached, and decisions made, prior to and as part of developing the business case, simply because they need to be included in the case for presentation to the decision makers. Not all the details will be known or needed yet; they can be further developed in the planning stage of the implementation, what I call phase zero. To make sure your proposal is going to be a winner, solicit the opinions of stakeholders and obtain their feedback and buy-in as early as possible. What follows is a short summary of some of the agreements required.

Agree the implementation approach

You need to agree how you will implement problem management, including whether it will be one group, area or technology at a time or all at once; which problems will be in scope and out of scope; and whether you will focus purely on reactive problem management or include proactive problems right from the start. To be convincing, the business case will need to address how the implementation will be carried out.

If you try to implement a fully functioning problem management function all at once, outcomes, and therefore benefit realisation, could be slow to develop, so a staged approach can often be a better choice. For a small organisation, a single implementation stage might be adequate, but for even slightly complex organisations, it makes sense to start small and build the function out over time, expanding the scope as momentum builds. Starting with one well-defined team, function, business group or location allows some immediate progress to be made and early results to be obtained. The approach can also be refined as lessons are learned about what works and what does not. There is the added advantage that you can compare results – for example the trend in incidents – between the implementation target and the 'status quo' organisation. The downside is that momentum might not develop and the full implementation might progress slowly past the initial phase or stall completely, becoming a niche function.

Other questions to ask are, if in stages, what are they and where will the implementation start? The business case and the draft plan need to set out how the implementation will progress, both in terms of scope (which areas, locations, functions, types of problems etc.) and the timetable for each project phase, together with costs and resources required.

Agree metrics and key performance indicators

It is vitally important to discuss, agree and set objectives for implementing problem management (real, business relevant and easily understood goals). To measure problem management effectiveness, these sort of up-front questions need to be asked:

- What actually needs to be measured and why?
- What targets should be set for each of the objectives?
- What mechanisms must be in place to capture the data and report on progress?
- What baseline data is needed before you start? In other words, what measurements about the current state need to be captured, so that there is a basis for comparison?
- What objectives and KPIs will be set for each project phase?
- How will progress and benefit realisation be measured? What should be achieved for each phase of the plan? This can be tough to agree and is covered in more detail in Chapter 3.

You might need to argue strongly for realistic and appropriate KPIs because my experience shows that measurements more applicable to incident management are often applied to problem management at the outset. Agreeing metrics is all about setting expectations correctly and then reporting back on how those expectations are being met. Chapter 7 addresses this topic in detail.

> The more granular you set targets, the simpler they are to manage against. For example, three lots of 20 per cent reduction are more achievable than one leap of 50 per cent, even though the result is the same: for 100 incidents, a 50 per cent reduction is 50 incidents. A 20 per cent reduction is 80, another 20 per cent is 64, and then another gets you to 51, so we are looking at the same outcome, more or less. Like any journey, it is much easier to see how you are tracking with a few regular milestones along the way.

In addition, it is usually unwise to set cautious or easy-to-achieve targets. Firstly, they will not build a sense of urgency to implement change. Secondly, management will not be convinced by easily met targets; more likely they will consider them as indicators of a lack of commitment or confidence to succeed. Thirdly, you do not need to be too cautious anyway. It might not be obvious at the outset, but experience shows that once problem management becomes embedded, the effects snowball and the outcomes tend to become quite significant. You will be quite surprised at what can be achieved, so setting conservative targets is unnecessary.

Agree the structure

The structure of the problem management function or team is discussed in detail in Chapter 5. For the business case, only enough detail is required to give an impression of the scale of the proposal and how the function will be resourced. These decisions include how many problem managers, if any, will be required in the first phases, whether they will come from within the current organisation or need to be recruited externally and what impact problem management will have on time and resources for the existing organisation.

In reality, the best structure for a given organisation only becomes apparent over time and how this develops will not be known at this stage. It might be sufficient to specify the proposed starting structure and the immediate resource requirements, noting that how the function develops will depend on how successful it is and how cost-effective it proves to be.

Agree the implementation plan

Given the structure, the implementation approach and measurements to track progress, you can then work out a high-level plan. While, for the business case, you only need to include enough detail to demonstrate that the proposal is well thought out and practical, it is well worth taking the trouble to talk through with stakeholders the objectives, the milestones, the schedule and the resources required, well before the business case is presented. As always, it is a matter of maximising the chances of success by getting some consensus before it gets in front of the decision-making body.

This chapter has discussed questions about problem management and the factors for success, so now the next chapter looks into how to construct the business case for implementing problem management.

3 DEVELOPING THE BUSINESS CASE

Before getting started on what goes into a business case, allow me to make some suggestions about how it might be structured. All organisations are different and a lot depends on your audience: is the business case aimed at your own team, your direct manager or senior management? If there is a standard template to use, naturally you should use it, whether it is short or long, in a report format, a table or a standardised PowerPoint® slide with key fields to fill in and so on. There is little point in preparing something that does not meet your management's expectations or their management's if that is to whom the business case will be presented. Check first and give your audience what they are used to.

If a report style is used, put the recommendation and value proposition at the front in an executive summary (one paragraph for a short case, maximum one page for a long one), and then develop your case. Avoid going through a lot of background, notes, options and costs before finally getting to a recommendation several pages in. Even if it is standard practice to follow that style, your audience will appreciate a short executive summary at the front, giving them the answers in brief to save their time and get to the point rapidly. I have provided more about structure at www.bcs.org/probmgt-extras with a couple of sample business cases that can be tailored to your situation, drawing together all the suggestions listed below.

Keeping these points in mind, from here on I will focus on the content of a business case for problem management.

The business case needs to answer the question 'Why should we introduce problem management?' It's a sales pitch, basically, so there is a need to set out the key selling points:

- the benefits to be gained from having problem management;
- why a structured approach is key to success;
- the value proposition in terms of costs and expected returns; and
- a proposed implementation plan, including the approach to managing organisational change, the communications plan and stakeholder management.

WHY HAVE PROBLEM MANAGEMENT?

The first objective is to convince the organisation to adopt problem management and use a systematic approach to prioritise and analyse problems, make decisions and handle complex issues. You should include a section on what it is – the 'features' in sales speak – and then go straight on to talking about the benefits. Use the information in Chapter 1 to set out the features.

The essential benefit of problem management is enhancing stability, which it achieves directly by fixing problems. By finding real root causes and resolving them completely, problem management addresses both actual and potential problems, reducing the number of:

- recurring incidents (remember the comparison with incident management previously); as well as
- hidden problems, which are incidents that haven't happened yet, but that would affect business operations if they did.

Problem management adds value by ensuring that problems are addressed comprehensively – meaning that it does not just deal with the immediate problem, but also identifies all instances of a technology, system or process that could be affected and in all regions or locations, and then implements solutions across all of them.

Indirectly, problem management impacts stability and reduces risk through being a positive influence on the design of applications, infrastructure systems and processes, and through improving the utilisation of resources by:

- reducing firefighting – which means more time for 'value-adding' work; and
- acting as a forum for collaboration across teams that might not normally work together.

In addition, regular reporting to management improves continual service improvement (CSI), ensures accountability for driving improvement and makes performance visible to all by putting KPIs in place to measure success.

WHY IS A STRUCTURED APPROACH TO PROBLEM MANAGEMENT REQUIRED?

A consistent and structured approach is a critical success factor, so persuading the organisation to adopt such an approach is an important part of the business case. The business case will be more successful if it includes benefits of the structured approach for both staff and management.

From a management point of view, working within a consistent and evidence-based framework:

- gives more certainty that the real problem has been addressed;
- introduces a common high standard of problem-solving skills;
- provides a method for assessing, resourcing and scheduling solution programmes, so that problems really get fixed;

- maintains clear visibility – status updates and problem reports give confidence that problems are being worked on and that progress is being made;
- leads to positive outcomes, namely:
  - a higher success rate and faster turnaround to solve problems;
  - information about problems being made available to help solve similar problems in future.

In the staff context (the people who will actually use the approach), a framework for problem-solving offers:

- more confidence when attacking problems, because teams know how to go about problem-solving. Skills training equips staff to focus on major problems – proactive, complex, cross-functional – the more common type of problem in many organisations.
- an evidence-based approach, which increases the certainty that the real problem has been fixed by:
  - asking precise questions to gather, sort, analyse and confirm information related to problems;
  - describing problems in specific terms to improve the chances of finding and confirming the true root cause; and
  - using a common language to improve communication.
- opportunities for improvement of services through analysing problem causes by type or category;
- an engagement model, which brings the right people together more easily to collaborate in solving and then fixing problems;
- a methodology with a common format for pooling information to allow problem managers to build and maintain close ties to SMEs in application and infrastructure teams, vendors and related process teams (for example capacity management, change and release management);
- skills to review data for trends and patterns to feed into proactive problem management for improving incident avoidance;
- consistent coaching and development for all staff;
- help for people to gain early successes, to build confidence and start to generate enthusiasm for a more structured, formal and ultimately more successful approach;
- clear visibility, which leads to confidence that all problems are being worked on and makes it easy to see who is working on what;
- happier customers and colleagues, increasing satisfaction through:
  - quickly sharing knowledge about problems;
  - working together across teams more easily;
  - a higher success rate and a faster turnaround; and
  - reporting automation replacing manual work.

In several implementations, I have found that even the most sceptical colleagues become enthusiastic champions after participating in a couple of successful structured problem investigations.

SETTING OUT THE VALUE PROPOSITION

The goal of this part of the business case is to explain the self-funding nature of problem management. Starting with the potential costs involved in setting up the function, you should next look at how to predict and set a return on that investment, then turn to the metrics required to confirm (or refute) that those returns cover and exceed the costs of running problem management.

Costs

It is important to consider and capture all the costs of implementing problem management because it presents a complete picture to the decision makers and strengthens your position by demonstrating that you have thought through all the implications. Costs fall into the two basic categories of one-off implementation costs and the ongoing costs to operate or run the problem management function.

Here is a sample list of the sorts of costs to consider. Naturally, not all will apply for every case and there might be others as well. Also, some costs fall into both one-off and ongoing cost categories.

Implementation project

- Project costs, such as: paying for a project manager, either appointed internally or hired externally; any dedicated or shared staff involved in the implementation team; other in-house or external resources, including any consultants used.

- Process development and documentation costs, such as engaging a technical writer or dedicating internal staff time to this task.

- Launch costs, commonly including the costs of any communications, new websites, staff and management briefings, newsletters etc.

Staff and resources

- Costs of staffing the function, such as: the recruitment costs of new problem managers if brought in externally; the opportunity costs of redeployed staff – what did existing staff stop doing to do problem management and how valuable was it?

- Any cost incurred through ongoing mentoring and support from external consultants or vendors that is not included in the implementation costs or tool licence and maintenance charges.

Training

Training costs are dependent on the level of training offered, whether basic or advanced, and who gets what and how much. This includes things like external accreditation and qualifications, if deemed appropriate. Of course, costs are also directly dependent on how many staff need to be trained.

Types of costs include:

- purchasing or developing training materials;
- running in-house or externally provided training sessions; and
- process and tool user guides and reference materials.

Tools

The cost of implementing problem management also depends on what tools are required, including whether there is a need to replace or enhance a current toolset or adopt a new system. Not using a tool at all can be cost-effective initially, but can also have adverse impacts on realising the benefits of problem management. Trying to keep track of problems manually, including their causes and the solutions implemented, quickly becomes unmanageable. It also makes sharing information with other teams more difficult, such as with the service desk or incident management.

If existing tools are to be used, consider:

- costs to modify or adapt; and
- additional licences, if required.

If a new tool is required, costs will include:

- the selection and evaluation process;
- implementation, hardware and/or hosting;
- software licensing and annual maintenance; plus
- support, including the ongoing development of enhancements.

Costs can be controlled by keeping modifications to a minimum, which is why existing features and workflows are an important consideration in the selection and evaluation of your toolset. Whether an existing tool or a new tool is used, there will also be training costs for staff to learn to use the tool in relation to the process you have adopted or designed.

Return on investment

There is no getting away from including a prediction of the return on investment (ROI) in the business case. The investment is the cost, effort and organisational change required, while the return is the benefit that problem management is expected to deliver. Regardless of how persuasive the case is otherwise, if management cannot see an adequate ROI, the proposal will not be approved. This section of the business case is where real business value is assigned to the results of implementing effective, structured problem management. While it is customary to express ROI in money terms, it does not necessarily have to be and I will cover both approaches here.

The aim is to take the proposed target for each KPI and link it to a real business outcome. Vague proposals that cannot be understood in real terms (e.g. 'improve stability by

10 per cent') are not good enough and will not be convincing. When talking to senior management, the value proposition must be concrete and expressed in real terms, so that it stands up to scrutiny. The key point is to express ROI in very specific business terms, using real examples from your own organisation. The process should be to:

- identify real concerns for your organisation that result from issues in the technology, application or business process area you are focusing on. Use the results from your survey and data gathering to pinpoint examples;
- express the impact as precisely as possible in terms that the business can understand;
- work out the improvement that should be seen if the specific, agreed problem management KPIs are met;
- set that as a goal against which problem management should be measured (and in what period).

Does that sound challenging? It should be. However, if you cannot come up with specific examples, the risk is high that problem management will not be adopted.

Working out the cost of down time

The best way to express value is in monetary terms. Although it is difficult to put a monetary value on incidents, there are a couple of approaches that can work. The first is to take a bottom-up approach and work from specific service interruptions. Ask business colleagues for an estimate of how much they might have lost when systems have not been available in the past. Here is an example:

> There have been 17 incidents in the past year that took the order processing system off-line for more than 30 minutes at a time. We received an average of 12 customer complaints per incident, including at least one cancelled order per incident and an unknown number of abandoned orders. The sales team estimates $27,000 of lost sales per incident. The cause of 12 of these incidents remains unclear. The head of sales predicts that a 25 per cent reduction in incidents affecting the order processing system should increase the number of orders processed successfully by 10 per cent year on year.
>
> By implementing more effective problem management, we can eliminate the underlying causes of these lost sales, as well as the 362 interruptions to other business processing in the last 12 months.

The example above is hypothetical, but modified from a real case. You might not know how much the 362 cost, but if you can get a real sample (like the example above) costed by your business colleagues, you can explicitly state that. This allows your audience to extrapolate for themselves the potential costs of the other 362 incidents. You get the dual advantages of winning your case and making the manager realise that you think of IT in terms of how it supports the business and the bottom line, in real money terms.

The second method is to take a top-down approach, which is a little more complicated to make convincing:

1. Take the overall revenue in a period (a year is often easiest to find out) for an organisation or a particular division. In other words, how much money they make.
2. Divide it by the number of minutes of business time in that period. This gives you an idea of how much each minute of processing time is worth to the business.

In other words, instead of working from specific incidents, you are attempting to derive a high-level estimate of the value that each minute of business activity is worth. Make your estimate quite conservative by reducing the value by a specified amount. The aim is to make it more acceptable and to acknowledge that system down time probably does not always lead to specific financial or business losses. Depending how conservative you want to be, halve the cost per minute, or even take a smaller proportion, like 20 per cent. If you work for a reasonable size organisation, it is still going to be a significant number.

Once you have this value, you can then make a reasonable case for how much incidents cost per minute of down time. From there you can show how much problem management can save, or how much additional revenue will be earned, for every incident that is resolved and will not happen again.

I have been fortunate to work for organisations where business units had already calculated these costs and you might find that, with a little effort, you might also be able to discover the information you need to make one or the other of these two methods work. If you need more information about calculating the cost of down time, there are many articles on the web. Two example articles are included in the references – one by (Martinez, 2009) and one by (Perlen, 2011).

In some cases, you will not have any solid data, either on value of down time or simply on the number of incidents and their duration. It might be that you are implementing service management in its entirety, so that incident management is not yet in place or not yet measured effectively. In this case, there is an alternative approach to demonstrating value that can also work quite well. For example, a survey run as part of deciding where you are starting from can include questions about customer concerns and issues (see Chapter 2). Even if the information is only anecdotal, it can be used for identifying real pain points and, from there, identifying what improvements would be considered valuable. This will involve talking directly to customers to understand their concerns in as much detail as possible and to build up a set of cases that need to be addressed.

Listing between five and 10 significant concerns, including how long they have been affecting customers, what impact they have and what sort of value is placed on removing them, can take the place of the cost analysis explained previously. In this situation, the business case might not be expressible in monetary terms; however, the benefits to be realised still need to be concrete and open to comparison with the costs of the proposal. Let me illustrate with an example:

The review of IT services for 2013 revealed the following concerns from business customers:

- Major systems are unreliable and experienced repeated failures during peak periods.

- There is little confidence that issues have been fixed, so there is an expectation that there will be similar impact to revenues during this year's peak.

- Customers feel that they are kept 'in the dark' and IT communicates poorly when things go wrong.

- When system upgrades occur or new business functionality is delivered, many features do not work as expected and the business always experiences failures, even in parts of applications that have not changed.

- There is a feeling that the impact of the failures outweigh the benefits from the new functions.

- The business does not believe that IT is taking any actions to change the current situation.

A list of concerns like this should generate a matching list of very specific benefits that problem management could help deliver for IT management:

- finding and fixing underlying causes;

- improving communications about what went wrong and how it is being addressed;

- reporting on the process improvements being implemented to reduce or eliminate failures following releases; and

- a timetable and action plan for delivering these improvements.

Measuring benefits and predicting outcomes

Once you have the costs and the hard benefits to be realised, the ROI can be shown. Remember that the objective is to explain the self-funding nature of problem management. This is the deal that is being struck: 'Give approval and this is what you will get in return.'

The measurements used in the business case also need to make it clear that there will be a timetable for realising benefits. Although there will be some instantaneous improvements from quick wins, the benefits will build up as the implementation progresses. One idea to show this is to have early targets set at lower levels, only becoming more ambitious over time. It is important to have realistic expected outcomes or benefits to be obtained for each milestone in the implementation plan, with target KPIs and metrics for each phase. Pay attention to 60-, 90-, 180-day milestones, and then annual performance targets, to show how success builds up, to help you see early success and to judge objectively whether you are on the right path in your implementation. Your proposal will not be successful if you are asking management to wait until the end to see benefits being realised.

THE PLAN

Including a plan for the implementation in project format is essential to the credibility of the business case. A plan says that you are serious about this, that you have thought it through and know how to go about realising the benefits you have outlined. It also helps maintain a sense of urgency and the momentum to drive forward. Although the plan need not be fully developed to the level required for implementation (which happens during the planning phase of the implementation), it should include:

- the implementation project structure, including the name of the sponsor and the budget;
- the implementation steps or phases;
- the metrics relevant to each phase;
- the schedule for benefit realisation; and
- a high-level communications and stakeholder management plan.

Project structure

By following standard project management methods, possible risks and obstacles can be identified and plans put in place to overcome them. Also, include a project team organisation chart showing the project sponsor, the project manager, coaches or consultants and who the implementers will be.

Implementation phases

The plan naturally needs to set out what will be done and what will be achieved in each phase of the project.

Phase zero

Often overlooked, the plan needs to include time to:

- sort out what the process and methodology will look like;
- develop the training plan – who will be trained in what and when;
- set measures to track the progress of the implementation project and the maturity of the process;
- write the communications plan – what people will be told at each stage of the implementation and how;
- decide where to start – probably the most important project success factor;
- decide how many stages are required if it is a large project for a large organisation and you need to proceed in stages;

- set the order of stages in the project – where you go next, the timing and how much overlap is required, if any; and

- collect baseline data to measure success against.

A common approach is to select or appoint a process owner, whose first job is to produce the phase zero plan. Remember, you do not need too much detail in the business case, but you need to lay out the milestones so your decision makers can see what will be delivered and when.

Further phases

Once it is clear where the process will be first implemented, you have identified the tasks in the plan, and you have thought through and agreed the process to be used, then you need to schedule phase one. This is the implementation phase for the first target group or location. Phase two then covers the consolidation phase of stage one plus starting phase one for stage two, then continuing to cascade until all target groups or locations are up and running.

Chapter 4 covers the details of all of the phases of the implementation project. It is necessary only to provide the high-level milestones in the business plan, but they should be very specific to your organisation and the time-frames need to be correct. The sample business plans at www.bcs.org/probmgt-extras should give you a good idea of how much detail is required.

Setting expectations in the business case for later phases strengthens the argument by making it clear that the plan is well organised and has every chance of success. By relating the target KPIs to each phase, it becomes clear whether the process is working, whether progress is satisfactory or too slow and whether doing structured problem management really is worth the cost.

The schedule

The plan included in the business case needs to give a clear, high-level picture of the time-frame envisaged and when and what benefits will be realised. Different time-frames will obviously suit different organisations and will depend on how much urgency needs to be generated. By including a timeline in the business case it will quickly become clear if the proposal is either too conservative or too aggressive, which allows you to adjust it to suit expectations before you start. At this point, there might need to be a discussion about implementation costs and resources, because a more aggressive timetable might take more resource effort and potentially will be more disruptive than a more methodical approach. You should expect the schedule to be very organisation-specific.

Stakeholders and communications

The stakeholder plan included in the business case does not need to show how to manage each stakeholder's expectations; all that is required is a sample list of stakeholders in order to acknowledge that stakeholder management planning will be done in phase zero. The communications plan – what messages, what media, who to, when and how often – probably needs a little bit more detail, just to make it clear what to expect. Include mention of the announcement of the implementation, including a message of support from senior management; the concept of a problem management 'launch' or roadshow at the start of phase one; and how regular progress updates will be delivered.

THE CALL TO ACTION

Like all good change initiatives, there is a need to generate a sense of urgency. The business case needs to finish with a summary of the benefits, a reminder of the proposed implementation start and end dates and a request for approval to proceed. Do not be concerned if you get a request for more analysis or a rework of some or all of the plan. This is almost as good as approval because it signals engagement and provides leverage for future commitment. Bringing back a revised plan that better meets expectations makes it harder for approval not to be given.

SAMPLE BUSINESS CASES AND PLANS

I have included two examples of business cases at www.bcs.org/probmgt-extras to give you a head start. The first is a document that pulls together all the content discussed in this chapter, including an executive summary and a call to action. The second is a more concise case, organised as a table. You can modify either to suit the style of business case most appropriate to your organisation. I have also included a sample implementation plan, based on two real-life projects at different organisations.

SECTION 2 – IMPLEMENTING AND RUNNING PROBLEM MANAGEMENT

4 THE IMPLEMENTATION PROJECT

This chapter is about the implementation project, its phases and staging. It is important to remember that when I say 'implementation' I do not mean you are starting from scratch. Handling problems is already happening in your organisation in some form and it might be good in some areas or quite ordinary overall. It might not have the title 'problem management' or be a separately identified activity or process. As long as you remember that your project involves at least some element of replacing what is already there, you can manage one source of unexpected resistance to change.

IMPLEMENTATION APPROACH

Implementation will naturally proceed in a series of phases, from start-up, through a consolidation period, and finally into a steady state or business as usual phase when problem management is fully embedded into the normal operating mode of the organisation. I introduced this idea in Chapter 3, while in Chapter 2 I also talked briefly about the idea of staging, which means with which group or area you are going to start, where you go next and the general order of implementing across an organisation. Staging is intended to break the implementation down into smaller chunks, to concentrate resources, learn and progress quickly and avoid the feeling that nothing is happening. Figure 4.1 might make the idea clearer.

Figure 4.1 A staged implementation

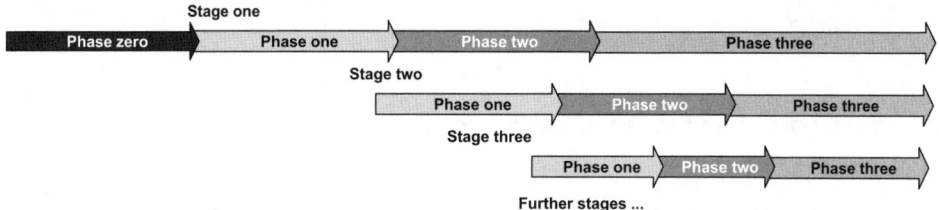

While you only do phase one once, a staged project is simply repeating the other phases as many times as you need to cover the whole organisation. You have probably already realised that each subsequent stage tends to accelerate through the phases, as more and more staff are trained and more successes are being seen.

In a small organisation, where the information services team is perhaps under 200 people, you can run the implementation as a single stage, but even then, you might like to consider a pilot team or technology area to start with, just to iron out the bugs in your process and approach to problem management.

PHASE ZERO: PLANNING AND PREPARATION

This is the planning phase, where all the preparatory tasks are done, including writing the project plan, setting the scope and approach, identifying key staff, developing the problem management process, putting together your training plan and materials, developing project and process metrics, and your initial project and process reporting content and frequency. A common approach to implementation is to select or appoint a process owner, whose first job is phase zero. This might well be your role.

Develop the detailed implementation project plan

Step one is to develop a detailed implementation plan. For a small implementation, you might find that the project template supplied at www.bcs.org/probmgt-extras is enough. Simply put in your dates and adjust the durations to suit. While you can build a larger project by repeating the sample plan through the stages, the level of complexity escalates rapidly and probably requires project management skills.

If you do not have any project management experience and your implementation is for a large organisation, a project manager will be an important asset, even if only part-time. If you are going to be the process owner and perhaps the lead problem manager as well, once you get into the implementation, you will quickly find you do not have enough time to manage the project as well. I have found that trying to do all three roles – project manager, process owner (which also includes chief trainer, process designer, stakeholder manager and evangelist) and primary problem manager – leads to, if not failure, then poorer outcomes or slower progress.

 Pick at most two roles out of process owner, primary problem manager and implementation project manager. For me, project manager is the easiest for which to find skilled people and safest to give up.

Design the problem management process

The second step is to design your problem management process. Do not fail to include time in the planning phase to sort out exactly what the process and methodology will look like, whether designed in-house or brought in through a vendor or external consultant. This is **not** about picking and implementing a tool, although that is also important; it is about making sure that you understand how you are going to go about investigating problems, finding their causes and implementing solutions to fix them. Section 3 of this book sets out a well-tested, reliable and effective process for doing problem management. It is fundamental to success to have a robust process in place from the beginning, so this step is essential and cannot be skipped.

If you bring in anyone from outside, a vendor or an external consultant, verify their practical experience. While theoretical expertise is valuable, if at all possible look for people who have actually done real-world problem management.

Set the scope for each phase

Setting the scope for problem management means determining which problems will be addressed and in which phases. Even in the smallest implementation, you cannot take on every problem investigation requested – you will not have the resources. It is essential to decide what types of problems you will take on and which ones you will not. Where you start will determine what category of problems you cover; however, you also need to be clear with your stakeholders what size problem or what percentage of problems you will cover in each phase and whether you will accept reactive problems only or proactive ones as well. The commonest approach I have seen is to take on only the highest priority problems in phase one (commonly referred to as major problems) and extend to include the next lowest priority in phase two.

I have run one large implementation where we covered only the highest priority problems related to IT infrastructure in phase one. For that organisation, this was plenty. For another smaller implementation, with only two problem managers (including me), we covered priority one and two problems across all applications, infrastructure and business areas. Actually, the scope was too large, because we lacked the resources to make consistent progress on the 200 or so problems raised in the first 12 months. It might have been better to narrow the scope somewhat to just priority one, until the process was embedded in the culture and people were engaged and able to drive investigation tasks and (especially) resolution activities, without constant supervision by the problem managers.

Do reactive problem management first, because that is how you learn to solve problems effectively in a repeatable way. Only after you and your team have experience and are successfully resolving problems using a well-structured method should you take on proactive problem management as well.

Decide the place to start

Phase zero also involves deciding where to start, including choosing a pilot group if required. The starting point evaluation depends on factors that are different for each organisation, especially on what is already in place and the level you are starting from, culturally and organisationally. Better results are obtained if you do the assessments covered in the first three challenges set out in Chapter 2. It might help to identify where the most pain is coming from and also which part of the organisation would be least resistant to adoption. It might be easiest to start the implementation in a willing location or one that has pressing needs. The upside of a well-delineated area is that success can be very easy to see and you can learn lessons quickly from doing the implementation.

The downside is that the next group might say, 'It was fine for them, but it cannot work for us, we're different.' I have experienced this reaction directly and it was necessary to demonstrate that problem management is the type of process that has wide applicability and that different areas are not all that different after all. Expecting this reaction in advance makes it much easier to deal with if it happens.

Almost all implementations will want to look for 'low hanging fruit' and quick wins, places where an immediate impact can be made and the concept can be proved. Nothing builds momentum better than success stories and positive outcomes early in the implementation. The most obvious marker for quick wins is the level of incidents. There might be a hot spot (hopefully not so hot that getting anyone's attention long enough to try to do problem management is impossible!) where the current team could be left in place fighting fires, while a separate team runs the new structured process, looking for root causes and applying fixes, even starting with just one problem. The result might be a rapid cool down and an immediate success, again something I have personally experienced. Of course, there is a slight risk that a quick win here might suddenly remove the sense of urgency to implement problem management. It all depends on how the outcome is presented to management.

However, the commonest ways for selecting a place to start are by business area, sets of applications and infrastructure or a location-specific approach. My first major implementation focused exclusively on infrastructure teams, because that is where I worked, leaving the (much larger) application area for stage two.

The best approach to selecting a place to start might be to choose a well-delineated area that has high numbers of high-impact incidents occurring. This sets you up for achieving a clear result by identifying and removing the causes of incidents and making a demonstrable improvement in stability in a relatively short space of time, provided the lessons set out in Chapters 5 and 6 are addressed.

Launch problem management

This new implementation needs a proper launch if it to be successful. In fact, it is one of the most important parts of phase one and needs to be fully planned in phase zero. By launch I mean a set of announcements, news items and introductory training sessions to raise awareness of what is coming, give stakeholders an idea of what problem management is about and build a sense of positive anticipation. Although the members of some organisations might be rather cynical of new initiatives, it is not an excuse to avoid this step.

While it is organisation-specific, I have found that there are several basic components to cover for every implementation launch. The basic elements are:

- incidents and problems – what's the difference?
- definition of problem management;
- difference from incident management;
- keys to success;

- advantages of structured problem-solving;
- benefits to the business;
- benefits to IT teams (what is in it for me, in other words);
- the 'rules of engagement' – how we work together, as well as the initial scope.

Assuming you use a slide deck, one slide on each topic is plenty. Remember to include the launch at the start of phase one for every new stage of a multi-stage implementation. An example of a launch pack that I have used successfully is included at www.bcs.org/probmgt-extras

I include the launch pack as the first few slides of the familiarisation training pack, covered in Chapter 5. I have found that after its initial use, this is how the launch is best incorporated, so that everybody hears the message again in training and new starters hear it as well.

Develop the training materials and delivery plan

Allocate time in phase zero to write or buy training materials. Remember, you need to prepare the familiarisation training for everyone who gets involved in problem management, as well as the specialist training for those people who will actually become problem managers. Work out all the logistics to organise the training sessions: who will be trained in what and when; track who has been trained; and how to report on progress. Delivering the training is time-consuming and is one of the reasons why a staged approach works best in an organisation of any size, because you only have to do one group or location at a time.

If the budget stretches, you might find it useful to bring in experienced coaches to lead training. Just make sure that you are in control of the content and agree with what these coaches include in the sessions.

Select and train the first problem managers

For phase one to get off to a good start and for problem management to be effective as early as possible, problem managers need to be trained and ready to go. This means that internal selection and/or external recruitment of problem managers is on the critical path of the project and so is their training, which needs to be finished in phase zero. Training and what makes a good problem manager are key topics of Chapter 5.

Set up the KPIs and metrics for phase one

It is a mistake to start implementing without any measurements in place. Use phase zero to set up the KPIs for the process, as well as the tracking measurements for the project. Your early success targets need to be implemented in parallel with the plan. KPIs and process metrics are about realising the benefits of problem management and you should have set out the high-level ones as part of the business proposal. Measurement is covered in Chapter 7, which also includes a method for implementing more challenging targets as the implementation progresses.

Measures to track the progress of the implementation and the maturity of the process as it develops are used during the project in both phases one and two, but several remain useful in a fully functioning organisation as well.

Pure implementation measurements include:

- numbers of staff trained;
- progress on recruitment; and
- the rate of increase in problems being managed under the process.

Those useful both during implementation and afterwards include:

- quality reviews and spot checks for adherence to the process;
- surveys to assess maturity and implementation progress; and
- opinion surveys on the current effectiveness of problem management.

You can measure all of these and report progress against planned targets. They are in addition to the hard metrics set out in Chapter 7. You need to score surveys for them to be an effective measure and you can assess process adherence by spot checks and quality reviews. You can also use testing results from training courses and numerical data extracted from your service management platform.

The rate of increase in problems being managed under the process has two uses. One aspect is concerned with tracking progress. The number of problems being investigated should steadily increase as more people adopt the process. If the rate of increase is slow, your implementation is probably not working well and you need to understand why and do something about it.

The other aspect is less obvious and is related to how you assess when you are moving from one implementation phase to another.

If you plot the numbers of new problems being raised each month, in phase one the trend will be upwards. In other words, more problems are being investigated each month as the process gets going. Once the graph levels off and the numbers of new problems are not increasing, you have reached phase two. When the numbers of new problems being raised starts to tail off or trend downwards, you know you have reached steady state, at least for that area of your organisation. (See Figure 4.2.)

Note that this is different from the numbers of new incidents being raised each month. Incident numbers and impact correlates more with the numbers of problems solved completely – cause found and a permanent fix implemented – and I will discuss this later when talking about error resolution.

Figure 4.2 Volume of open problems

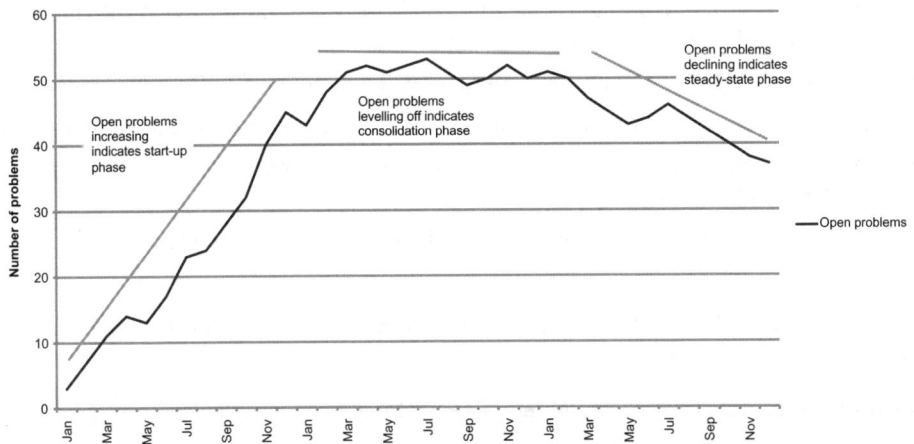

Also design your reporting framework – which metrics and KPIs will be reported to whom and how often. This is closely linked to your communications plan and will need to be tailored to what your management and the wider organisation expects. Chapter 7 also gives more on this.

Make sure that the implementation milestone targets match the planned activities at each phase. The capability to achieve a target must be in place before you are being held accountable for meeting it. For example, investigation teams have been engaged and trained before the target for time to find root cause is in operation. The plan should be tested against the proposed targets: walk through to check that wherever the plan and the targets meet up, the necessary actions have taken place to give the organisation the capability to deliver against the targets set. It is not that difficult if the plan is well constructed, with milestones that can be matched to the progressive metrics that are supposed to be measuring the development of the function.

Wherever you start, it is important that baseline data is available, including current numbers and severity of incidents, availability measurements, number of applications and so on. You can only track success against the targets and timelines you have set for your first phase if you know from where you started.

Prepare the project communication plan

As I have mentioned previously, the communication plan is all about telling what to who and when. I covered the importance of effective communication as a factor for success in Chapter 2. Phase zero of the implementation is where you actually map out the details of the plan.

In the business plan, all that is required is:

- an announcement that problem management is to be introduced, along with the expected benefits noted previously;
- where and for whom problem management will be launched first;
- information about familiarisation training being rolled out to all impacted staff;
- confirmation that regular updates on progress, including problems investigated in the new process, will be given; and
- assurance that a specific (hopefully pre-existing) forum will be used to report progress.

Before phase one of the implementation you need to have set out in detail all the following:

- the actual communications targeted to each stake holder group;
- the schedule of communication; and
- the channels to be used.

A communication channel is a commonly understood term. For clarity, in this book it refers to the method and forum used for talking to each stakeholder group and for each specific type of communication. For example, you might decide that the best way to reach technical teams with updates is through an existing discussion forum, such as an internal Yammer platform, while for managers it is via a regular agenda item at their management meeting. For both, you might want to make major announcements through an existing staff newsletter or the department home page.

Table 4.1 is a sample communication plan.

Table 4.1 A sample communication plan

Communication type	Audience	Channel	Frequency
Announce problem management	All staff in the IT or IS organisation	News article, home page announcement, segment at an all-staff 'town hall' meeting	Once
Show management support	All staff in the IT or IS organisation	'Talking head' video by a senior manager	Once for every phase one of the project

Table 4.1 (Continued)

Communication type	Audience	Channel	Frequency
Launch problem management	Staff in the target group or location	'Roadshow' or face-to-face briefing session, backed up by web-ex or similar (less effective)	Once for every phase one of the project
Implementation progress updates	All staff in the IT or IS organisation or limit to target group (depends on organisational culture)	Yammer bulletins, newsletters, scorecard on department website, management briefings at an existing management forum	Minimum of every two weeks
Announce wins and successes	All staff in the IT or IS organisation or limit to target group (depends on organisational culture)	Yammer bulletins, newsletters, news item on department website	As often as possible, every time a major problem is solved or a breakthrough is made in an investigation
Formal management reporting	Management, however defined (also share all management reporting with your problem management team)	Initially, existing management forums and established reporting structures. By phase two, through dedicated problem management reporting forums as well	Weekly or monthly, depending on what is already in place

You could also include regular formal project reporting and decision points in the communication plan, it is up to you. I prefer to keep it as simple as possible and just cover the basics, leaving reporting and requests to proceed as project tasks and milestones.

Put individual and repeating tasks in the project plan for each of the main communications to make sure they happen.

Prepare the stakeholder management plan

A stakeholder management plan is essentially a list of all your stakeholder groups (usually not individuals, unless it is important to single out a role like the chief information officer (CIO)), specifying what their 'stake' is in problem management. For example, are they necessary to help the process happen; do they support the implementation project; do they benefit from the process; do they provide approvals to proceed or spend money and so on? You then have to assess whether each group is likely to be hostile, supportive or neutral and what is required to manage each one.

When selecting stakeholders, ask questions like:

- Who have been or will be the biggest critics?
- Who are my customers?
- Who do I need to win over to make the project succeed?

The list needs to be comprehensive. Missing a key stakeholder group can limit the success of your implementation. It is worth brainstorming the list of stakeholders and their expected attitudes with your team, or a group of trusted colleagues, to minimise this risk.

Make a regular time to review the stakeholder plan, to highlight any groups that have changed their attitudes, positively or negatively, or need more or less attention or a change in how their relationship is being managed.

Like the communication plan, a table is often the simplest way to keep track (for example Table 4.2)

This is just an example, but is not very different from an actual stakeholder plan I have used. Note that the stakeholder plan is probably not a public document, because people might not like to feel they are being 'managed' and their attitudes are being assessed.

Put in a line in your plan for every separate resolver group you rely upon. For example, include the UNIX team, the network team, the finance application support team and any other teams in your IT department. Do the same for your key vendors, outsource partners and each development team. By separating out each group, you can deal with different attitudes, whether supporters, active detractors or uncommitted.

Confirm how problems are raised for investigation

The final thing to do in phase zero is to make sure that you have a definite agreement about how problems will be raised, especially with the incident management team (if you have one) and the service desk. See Chapter 11 for more on this subject.

Table 4.2 A sample stakeholder management plan

Stakeholder	How affected/ affecting	Attitude	Management plan
Resolver group A	Provides technical knowledge and resources, receives support from structured process, problem management competes for resource time	Resistant to change	Familiarisation training, assign credit for fixing problems, hold accountable for engagement
Resolver group B	Provides technical knowledge and resources, receives support from structured process, problem management competes for resource time	Enthusiastic supporters	Familiarisation training, assign credit for fixing problems, hold accountable for engagement
IT management team	Provides resources, support and approvals, demands answers, cost containment and improvements to services	Cost and risk averse, not yet convinced about value	Keep fully informed, report failures as well as successes, assign credit to resolver groups at all times
Incident management team	Benefits from reducing incidents, competes to own the benefits	Grudging acceptance	Maintain regular dialogue and commit to collaborate
Service desk	Benefits from solutions and knowledge, finds trends and patterns pointing to problems	Enthusiastic supporters	Maintain regular dialogue and commit to collaborate
Change management team	Provides structure to implementing solutions, benefits from improvements to team attitudes and work practices	Enthusiastic supporters	Maintain regular dialogue and commit to collaborate
Vendor A	Provides solutions, receives money	Resistant to change	Work through vendor management

(Continued)

Table 4.2 (Continued)

Stakeholder	How affected/ affecting	Attitude	Management plan
Vendor B	Provides solutions, receives money	Enthusiastic supporters	Work through vendor management
Outsource provider A	Provides solutions, can hide problems, resists spending money to resolve problems	Grudging acceptance	Work through vendor management
Outsource provider B	Provides solutions, can hide problems, resists spending money to resolve problems	Cooperative as long as it costs them nothing	Work through vendor management
Customer group A	Demands stable services, benefits from reduction in incidents	Not specifically aware of problem management	Ensure IT management and service managers have full information at all times
Development team A	Provides solutions, manages conflict for resources and priorities	Resistant to change	Familiarisation training, assign credit for fixing problems, hold accountable for engagement
Development team B	Provides solutions, manages conflict for resources and priorities	Grudging acceptance	Familiarisation training, assign credit for fixing problems, hold accountable for engagement
Problem management team	Provides problem-solving skill, deals with conflicts, benefits from satisfaction of making a difference	Non-committal	In-depth training, support and coaching, acknowledge successes and work through failures
Vendor management	Receives feedback about vendor performance, holds vendors accountable	Mild supporters	Maintain regular dialogue and commit to collaborate

PHASE ONE: START-UP

Phase one is the start-up phase. The focus is on forming the team and publicising the process. Incident and problem management should also implement their agreement about working together, including handing-off from one process to the other and how to manage communications.

The key elements of phase one are described in the following sections.

Launch problem management

The first thing to do is to execute your launch plan for problem management, to make sure people know what problem management is and why you are implementing it. This part of your communications plan must happen before everything else.

Announce coverage and starting point

Problem management should only cover the scope set in phase zero. Clearly state which types and priorities of problems will be investigated during phase one. It might be best to specify this in your launch package. There should not be any need for further discussion about scope at this point because you should have already agreed this in phase zero. Also, for a staged implementation, include the specific area you are focusing on for this stage. By setting this out, you make it easier to turn down problems that are out of scope in phase one.

There will be pressure to take on more problems than you can handle. However, your resources are already fully committed and you need to resist scope creep at this early point in the project.

I suggest that you should not be too worried if you are being asked to take on additional problems – it is proof of success if people want to take advantage of the structured problem management you offer. It might indicate that it is time to implement phase two in the area where you are currently operating. If the problems being proposed are coming from a different area, perhaps it indicates that you are ready for the next project stage as well, targeting this new area.

Implement the process for requesting problem investigations. You are starting with reactive problem management, so this mainly means initiating the agreed handover from the incident management process.

Run familiarisation training

The largest and most labour-intensive task in phase one is running familiarisation training. It is vital to make sure everyone receives this training. Report regularly on progress and clearly highlight any teams or individuals who resist the training or continually find excuses not to attend. People should not be invited to engage in problem analysis unless they have done the training because it means time will be wasted time with explanations during investigation sessions.

Launch the communications and stakeholder management plans

Deliver against the plans you have put together to get the benefits. Commit at this early stage to follow through on the communication plan and the project will be much more successful, as well as be seen to be successful. Revisit your stakeholder management plan not only at regular intervals, but also every time you meet resistance, or the project does not seem to be going according to plan. I have found that referring to the stakeholder management plan and revising it as necessary helps maintain focus, identify when circumstances have changed, both positively and negatively, and therefore when the approach for certain groups also has to change.

Start solving problems

Jump in and run your first problem investigations. Nothing succeeds like success. As soon as you have buy-in and a structured method sketched out (it does not need to be fully developed), agree to run a problem entirely in the new method. If you are not already experienced in problem investigation techniques, you might want to consider using an expert consultant to run this first one to help improve your chances of success. Track the progress of the investigation, note all the difficulties in using the process and report successes. This is a good opportunity to look for a contrast between the new method and existing practices:

- Was it faster to find the cause?

- Were all the issues and contributing factors clearly understood and articulated?

- How well did teams engage and collaborate to solve the problem?

Take measurements and start reporting

Based on the metrics worked out in phase zero and in the business plan, start reporting on both the implementation project and the problem management process at a suitable management forum. The first step is to capture the baseline data that was agreed, so you have something to compare against as you start to measure the developing maturity of the process.

While it is natural to prefer reporting on success, it is important for the credibility of problem management that you also report difficulties, delays and failures. Also remember that, in phase one, the numbers of problems being raised and investigated tends to increase month by month, so this should be seen as normal.

Transition to phase two

At some point, phase one reaches a natural conclusion and phase two commences. This is usually not a clean break because one phase normally cross-fades into the other. You cannot easily represent this in a project plan that management would find acceptable. The best you can do is to set a specific time-frame, perhaps six to nine months at most, for when a milestone is reached to assess progress and make a go/no-go decision to move to the next phase. If you are doing a staged implementation, and if it has not already happened earlier, the decision should also be made now to start phase one of stage two, with the next group or area to be targeted.

Remember Figure 4.2, the graph of the volume of open problems. The best indicator of when phase one is finishing and phase two is commencing is when the rate of increase in the number of problems under investigation starts to level off from its upward trend.

The crossover between starting up and moving into consolidation of the operation should also include a decision point about whether progress has been satisfactory. Optimistically, the implementation should be sufficiently successful that the decision to continue is a formality, but it is prudent to consider at least that success might be more limited than expected. The metrics should tell the story clearly either way and, if you are not hitting your targets, this is the point to pause and review, apply your problem management skills to understand the causes and formulate plans to recover the situation. Revisit your stakeholder management plan, because, most often, lower than expected outcomes will link back to organisational culture and resistance to change.

PHASE TWO: CONSOLIDATION

The consolidation phase is all about ensuring that the actions planned in phase zero and implemented in phase one are embedded, and that the specific enhancements that are planned for phase two are introduced successfully. The rate of new problems being raised levels off and it is time to review the implementation thoroughly and make improvements where necessary.

Stages

If the decision is made to go to the next stage, extend problem management to cover the next targeted areas, technologies, applications, support groups, customers and priority of problems. This is where the benefits of a staged approach are realised. You are able to leverage successes from the start-up phase when you extend the service into new areas. You can reuse training, demonstrate the most effective behaviours from the existing implementation and lend problem managers to leverage their experience.

Alternatively, if the next stage is postponed, the reasons should be clear and consolidation of what you have achieved so far will be even more important. Once the implementation is back on track, you can reconsider moving to phase two.

One thing to watch out for when using the existing implementation as a model is the type of resistance in which groups or locations use arguments like:

- the initial implementation area was a mess and needed fixing, but we are fine and we do not need problem management; or
- that stuff might work for you, but it cannot work here because we are different.

In these cases, the approach is not unlike when you started in phase one, stage one, because there are organisational issues to be overcome and you have new stakeholders. A revised stakeholder management plan is required and the launch might need to be tailored to address any specific concerns.

Scope

Consolidation also covers extending the scope of problem management to take on more and different types of problems. If your phase one scope was only to cover major problems, you could start to develop a process to take up lower priority problems as well. This is a major deliverable of phase two.

Your experience is likely to parallel a very common pattern: the big problems are being taken up for investigation, but there are no resources or insufficient time available to pick up smaller problems, so a backlog builds up. This issue can be addressed without building a large team of dedicated problem managers to cover more problems because there are two factors involved and two actions you can take.

The first is to take a small number of problem managers away from major problems to review the problems you have logged, as well as your process for raising problems. This can be done by just one problem manager or, if one problem manager is all you have, they can dedicate a small but regular percentage of their time to minor problems, say 10 per cent.

I regularly see problems raised whose cause can be linked to investigations already in progress. You can then put these problems on hold. In many cases, you will find that the solution of the first problem addresses this new problem as well, or that only a small amount of work is required to modify the solution in order to resolve the new problem.

The second approach is based on the nature of minor problems. In general, minor problems are quite limited in scope. They do not need investigation by a cross-functional team because the fault area is limited to one technology or one application. In these situations, the problems can be assigned to SMEs from that area. With a little coaching from an experienced problem manager, and perhaps some refresher training, this can be a very successful approach to minor problem investigation.

Connections

During this phase you should ensure that all the processes that problem management depends on have the required connections established and include the features needed for success. The key ones include knowledge management and change management; however, because the main focus has been on reactive problem management, incident management is the most important. The handover from incident to problem management must be well understood and working smoothly.

By the time you get to phase two, you might find that a common criticism is that 'solving problems takes too long'. Several factors are involved here, including the level of engagement with your resolver groups and the effectiveness and efficiency of your structured investigation methodology. One common source of delay is that problems sit for too long waiting to be picked up for investigation. Generally, this points to a lack of resources.

The effectiveness of handover can also be a significant factor. For example, in one implementation I ran in a larger organisation, problems were being logged without the problem team knowing about them. The solution was to tighten up the handover process to reinforce the acceptance step and to monitor unassigned problems regularly in order to highlight orphaned requests. I cover the incident-to-problem interface in Chapter 11.

Knowledge management is a very useful process for problem management because the knowledge base provides a repository of information that is useful for understanding problems and looking for solutions. It also serves as a place to record root causes, workarounds and solutions for future reference. If there is no effective method in place for managing useful information, phase two is a good place to start working with colleagues and management on managing knowledge more effectively (see Chapter 6).

Along with incident management, **change management** tends to be the first process to develop in most organisations. It integrates closely with problem management and is usually well developed by the time this phase of your implementation is reached. The connections to review and improve, if necessary, are:

- whether a method is available to identify the changes that have occurred in a particular time period or to a particular component of the environment;

- whether the assessment of change planning, implementation and verification is being done by the change team and results are available for review. This is essential when identifying root causes of problems because without it, it can be difficult to trace back to understand why a particular problem occurred; and

- whether the change process can be depended upon to ensure that problem solutions are implemented properly and without creating new problems.

If available, **configuration management** supplies essential information needed to solve problems effectively. In particular, the configuration management system should be able to supply up-to-date information about a given system, including components, relationships, dependencies, versions, maintenance status and all the other elements needed to describe the system.

Review process, technology and structure

To keep the momentum going as problem management becomes a normal part of the organisation, constant review and improvement is essential. You should assess how the process is working, as well as the organisation structure, staff capabilities, roles and responsibilities and the technology being used to support problem management.

It is not enough to ensure you have a process in place that aligns to ITIL® best practice. Every step needs to be assessed to look for bottlenecks, things that do not make sense or add no value and, mainly by talking to your stakeholders, steps that might be inflexible or missing altogether:

- Is problem management delivering what you committed to deliver?

- Are you on track in terms of planned outcomes at this phase of the implementation?

- ▪ If not, is the process itself part of the problem?
- Are you finding root cause regularly and in the agreed time-frames?
  - ▪ If not, is the structured analysis procedure you have adopted faulty or too slow?
- Are problems being resolved in a reasonable time-frame?
  - ▪ If not, do you have enough structure and measurement around the implementation of solutions?

Phase two is also a good time to make sure that your approach to organising the problem management function is meeting requirements (see Chapter 5) – is it working as planned? Your metrics should be telling you this. If you are not meeting targets and the process appears to be well defined, the assessment should turn to the people, who does what, how they work together and how capable they are:

- Have any work practices crept in that are working against your objectives?
- Is everyone following the process in the same way?
- Do problem managers have the right level of skills and the right attitude to be as successful as possible?
- Are there enough skilled resources available to be effective?

By now, you should be able to get a good impression of how engaged your SMEs are as well. (For simplicity, apart from problem managers, I refer to everyone else who gets involved in problem management collectively as SMEs, see Chapter 5). It is important to identify those that are effective and supportive and those that are not:

- If some teams are better engaged than others, what can be learned to improve and standardise the SME engagement model across all groups?
- If your model leads to some SME groups always engaging through the same problem managers and, if there are differences in performance, is it the SME group or is it the problem manager?
- Do individual problem managers get better results when dealing with one SME group than with another?

When running a staged implementation, these reviews should be applied to areas in the different stages as well. Adherence to your process should be compared across all groups, using assessments such as performance against KPIs, but also against more subtle measures, such as how well unresolved problems are handled.

This is also a good time to revisit how you are classifying your problems in terms of root causes. If, like most implementations, you start with the coding system predefined in your toolset, or inherited from incident management or a pre-existing problem management methodology, you will almost certainly want to implement better root cause codes at this point. I feel strongly about this subject and discuss an effective model in Chapter 6.

Finally, review your tool requirements because it is likely that you will be making improvements to your toolset all the time for better workflow, better monitoring and reporting, better analysis and data gathering, better knowledge and better system information. Now is a good time to look at the toolset overall, to identify any gaps and to improve capabilities where required.

Phase two is not just about expanding the scope and taking on more problems, it is also a time to review and improve what was implemented in phase one. Phase two builds on phase one in other ways as well, particularly in improving quality, skills and how you manage solutions, but also by improving governance and extending your organisation's proactive problem-solving capabilities.

Quality

The quality of outcomes from problem management can be enhanced by putting process monitoring in place. By this I mean the ability to track problems throughout the workflow to make sure that detection, logging, prioritisation and all the other steps are efficient and to identify quickly bottlenecks or delays in the process. Section 3 suggests a set of useful parameters to implement. Quality should also be measured in terms of the usefulness of the information recorded about problems, such as how well causes are described and the clarity of descriptions of solutions implemented (see Chapter 6).

Simple things like the use of follow-up dates and reminders can be very effective to keep problem managers and SMEs on target. This is also a good time to look at more complex measurements, like workload monitoring, staff and counterparty feedback mechanisms and formal customer satisfaction surveys.

At this point, most implementations would not have established a fully effective communication model. Most implementations start with manual preparation of status reports, formal problem reports, KPI measurement and management reporting. Phase two gives you the opportunity to make these more efficient by automating as much as possible, giving time back to your problem managers to make best use of their investigation and problem-solving skills.

I have found that introducing more granularity into prioritisation also improves quality outcomes by ensuring the most important problems are addressed first and others are scheduled appropriately. Once a solid workload of problems builds up, you will have multiple problem investigations to progress that are all at the same priority. Of 50 problems, you might have 10 at priority 1, 15 at priority 2 and 25 at priority 3. There is a natural tendency for people to pick and choose what they work on. A second level of prioritisation can help rank problems of the same overall priority and ensure the highest risk problems are getting the attention they deserve. See Chapter 12 for more details. In addition, ranking lower priority problems, which by their nature might not attract the management attention of higher profile ones, helps to ensure that the most important of these are addressed first.

Skills

In phase one, you trained your problem managers and everyone else who engages in the process. This training needs to continue and should be embedded in the on-boarding process in order to prevent the process's effectiveness being watered down and to bring all problem managers to a common level of practice. The most effective problem managers should be reviewed to identify the key factors in their success. Lessons learned should be applied to improve the common practice of the whole problem management team. Also consider refresher training and, if you have adopted one of the formal frameworks, consider offering the next level of qualification in that framework to your senior team members.

In a staged deployment, the focus should be on bringing skills in each target group up to a consistent level as each passes into phase two in turn. Regular self-assessment by the problem management leads for each area should show how they compare against whichever area has reached the highest level of maturity.

Problem advisory board

Phase two is the best time to set up and start running the problem advisory board, the PAB. Problem management should be sufficiently understood by now so that the purpose of the PAB can be readily explained and the right membership and working model adopted. The PAB is needed now because it is a very good way to put structure and governance around the selection of proactive problems and can provide the authority to drive the implementation of solutions. How to set up and run the PAB is covered in detail in Chapter 5.

Launch proactive problem management

Now that sufficient skills and experience have built up from investigating reactive problems, extend the scope by introducing formal proactive problem management. At this stage, problem managers will already be looking for potential problems and at least some proactive problem investigations will be occurring (for more information see Chapter 11).

The process for requesting problem investigations also needs to expand, so that it becomes the mechanism for people to suggest problems. A useful selection method is to use the PAB to review proposals, choose which ones to pursue and then prioritise them appropriately. Some might be put on hold until suitable resources are available and some will be rejected. The reasons why specific problems are held over or rejected should be clearly documented and communicated back to the proposer.

Managing solutions

By now, you have probably noticed that some problems get fixed promptly and some seem to take forever to have the agreed solutions implemented, if at all. To be effective, you not only need to find the cause, you also have to implement a solution to prevent it happening again. Doing one without the other is useless. The PAB is also a good mechanism for managing and monitoring the delivery of problem solutions, as discussed in Chapter 5.

In addition, now is a good time to establish a protocol to handle large-scale resolution initiatives, those that are essentially major projects.

PHASE THREE: STEADY STATE

In a steady-state operation, the rate of new problem investigations raised will naturally start to decline, simply because of the success of problem management in removing the sources of instability from the environment. Steady-state problem management focuses mainly on proactive problem management and looking towards future potential sources of problems. I have to say that I have yet to experience an organisation that has reached this steady state. I think this is simply because problem management has tended to lag behind other functions such as incident and change management.

Extend the reach of problem management

Successful problem management should mean that there are fewer problems to manage, implying that fewer problem managers will be needed. One option for using this spare capacity could be to extend the reach of problem management outside IT and even outside the organisation. I turn to these possibilities in Chapter 9.

Vendor standards

There is a need to ensure that the introduction of new vendors is not detrimental to your problem management capabilities. A common experience is that outsourcing support to a vendor organisation re-introduces sources of instability that had been eradicated. These can include poor adherence to change practices, less robust coding standards or testing regimes and lower quality monitoring of production systems.

To ensure that new sources of problems are minimised, the problem management function should seek a seat at the table during vendor assessment and contract negotiation. Any new vendor contracts should give rights to enforce effective problem management through clearly defined responsibilities and effective tracking of tasks and actions.

Dealing with vendors can lack transparency. The organisation and the vendor will have different priorities and agendas and there might be a strong motivation not to reveal information, especially about a known problem or one that relates to a central or key element of the service offering from the vendor. These attitudes are by no means universal, but it is important that problem managers keep in mind the possibility that a conflict of interest might be clouding the situation.

This has been a long and detailed chapter, but its subject is one of the core objectives of this book. Success is driven by careful consideration of all these factors and I hope you now appreciate that careful planning is of the highest importance. Chapters 5 and 6 go more deeply into how to organise your teams and the critical success factors for running problem management.

FURTHER READING: ORGANISATIONAL CHANGE ISSUES

The topic of resistance to change is important to any implementation; however, it is a topic that is too large to cover in detail in this book. Instead, here are some references that you might find useful.

The first two are short articles from the *Harvard Business Review* and are both classic articles from very influential authors in this field. Many organisations have access to this journal; otherwise the articles are very inexpensive to purchase online and can be downloaded from http://hbr.org/:

Kotter, J.P. (1995) Leading change: Why transformation efforts fail. *Harvard Business Review*, 73 (2). 59–67.

Garvin, D.A. and Roberto, M.A. (2005) Change through persuasion. *Harvard Business Review*, 83 (2). 104–112.

A short book that I have found extremely useful is from the 'Go MAD thinking' group. It is, at most, 70 pages of content and summarises all the key elements of organisational change:

How to save time and money by managing organisational change effectively (Gilbert and Hutchinson, 2009)

Lastly, if you want to read the classic (now with a new preface by the author) on the subject:

Leading change (Kotter, 2012)

5 ORGANISING PROBLEM MANAGEMENT AS A FUNCTION

This chapter is about running problem management. It covers four related topics:

- How to organise your problem management function in terms of team structure, for both small and large organisations.
- The people you need in the team, who else needs to get involved and what skills and training are required.
- How to structure and run the main process elements of root cause analysis and resolution, including effective communication throughout the process.
- How to run an effective governance model – the PAB.

THE ORGANISATIONAL MODEL USED

Deciding how to structure the problem management function is a challenge for both small and large organisations. Some things are common, such as how to engage with SMEs, and overall team size is more or less a function of the organisation's size and complexity. However, the centralised versus decentralised question is a burning issue for large organisations that does not arise in small ones, where the core issue is whether one problem manager is enough and what that person actually does.

The only definition I have for 'large' is in terms of complexity. A large organisation will typically have multiple business lines supported by a complex and diverse set of applications, with some specialised to a particular business and some 'enterprise' or standard across all. IT staff might be located centrally or in multiple locations and support both these multiple applications and an IT infrastructure that can be very uniform and standardised, different for every business line with little standardisation or somewhere in between. All functions might be outsourced to one or more vendor organisations or there might be a mix of in-house and vendor sourcing, depending on requirements.

A small organisation typically has one or a small number of business lines and is limited to a single location or a small number of sites. They can still have global reach through technology, of course. The IT staff are concentrated into a few specific teams in one or several locations. There might be up to 1,000 staff in total and perhaps between 50 and 200 IT staff at most.

In between are organisations of every size and shape. I am going to talk mainly about the two ends of the spectrum: a large, multi-divisional and perhaps international organisation, which has multiple problem managers, and a small-to-medium firm, which might also cover a typical provincial or local government department, with one or two problem managers, or even none at all. The suggested models are scalable (up and down), so that an organisation that is somewhere in between these two extremes should be able to use the guidance to implement an effective function as well.

Problem management in large organisations

Depending on their maturity, large IT teams will have service management staff dedicated to all the specialties. Almost all will have an incident management team and a change management team. Setting up a team of problem managers as well will seem a natural and acceptable step. For example, most organisations have a single change management team to own the overall process and coordinate a unified view of changes across the organisation, although there might be dedicated change managers in each division and individual change advisory boards for each. Similarly, you will usually find a single incident management team whose job is to manage major incidents wherever and whenever they occur, or a 'team of teams' in different locations for different business lines and technology platforms.

Problem management can be organised in several ways, but the most common discussion I have observed is whether it is better to run one centralised problem management team or to distribute individual problem managers throughout the organisation, dedicated to specific business lines or sets of technologies.

The centralised versus decentralised decision

The challenge for setting up a problem management function is to provide a high performance problem management team while ensuring effective customer alignment. To achieve this efficiently and effectively, a working model and organisation structure is required that can provide this coverage without the need for excessive numbers of problem managers.

- **Decentralised problem management –** Placing individual problem managers or small teams into specific areas has the advantage that the problem managers become part of the wider support team and get to know the people, the business itself and the systems and processes that support that business area very well. They are able to deliver focused customer service to meet that division's customer expectations. There are a few disadvantages, however:

  - Dedicating problem managers to specific areas is not very efficient and can be inflexible in terms of distributing workload. Some areas will have a significantly higher workload than others and, because dedicated problem managers have a fixed capacity to take on problems, there could be situations where one area is overwhelmed while problem managers in other areas are not particularly busy.

  - It can open up single points of failure. When staff take leave, there is a risk that individual problem managers will not have a suitable back-up person who has developed experience with the systems, processes, applications and people in a given area.

- A distributed model is liable to undermine a consistent, high quality, structured approach to solving problems. Unless great care is taken to make sure it does not happen, it is highly likely that individuals working in their own areas will develop their own approaches to solving problems – some good, some less effective. Standards might decline and the opportunity to share good ideas and improvements with other problem managers might be lost.

- Most significantly, in this structure, it is challenging to provide collaborative, multi-disciplinary problem-solving across teams. It makes it more difficult to investigate problems that impact more than one area or have causes that lie outside the area that the problem manager normally covers. Collaborative team engagement is not the norm in a distributed problem management model. A mechanism is required to ensure that the need for cross-functional engagement is recognised when dealing with complex problems that span organisational boundaries.

- **Centralised problem management** – Running a central team responsible for managing all problems has the advantage of maintaining high standards, through the coaching and peer review that comes from all problem managers working together. It makes the pool of problem managers larger, making it easier to cover for staff leave and allocate resources effectively to the busiest areas. In particular, it makes it easier to investigate problems that are more general or span the boundaries between areas.

  The disadvantage is that, without specialisation in one area, problem managers will maintain good problem management skills, but not develop as thorough an understanding of each division's people, processes, systems and specific business needs as they would in a decentralised structure. Without this knowledge and expertise, and especially without good relationships with the people involved, the effectiveness of the problem process can be impacted. A lack of confidence might develop concerning whether problem managers are really able to help solve an area's problems and can limit the acceptance and effectiveness of the process.

A federated solution

I have found that a federated model combines the strengths of both approaches while minimising the weaknesses. A federated model is based on maintaining a central team and also having problem managers dedicated to individual business areas. Good outcomes can be achieved by enforcing adherence to a common process and by putting adequate structure and governance in place. There are two ways of realising a federated approach and I have seen both work effectively.

One arrangement is for a central team to be the 'owners' of the core problem management process and expertise, highly trained in structured problem-solving techniques and able to train and coach less experienced team members. The central team could all sit together, which would be ideal for an organisation with one main location, or could be distributed into small teams across several locations. The problem managers distributed or embedded in the support teams for the individual business divisions handle problems in their own areas, but rely on the central team for additional expertise in problem-solving, for maintaining uniform standards and to act as an escalation point to coordinate problems that cross divisional boundaries. This can be an appropriate arrangement for very large organisations, provided the workload of the isolated problem managers can be managed effectively and gaps can be filled to cover leave and single points of failure.

This model requires an effective oversight and governance model, with rules and limits, so people know which problems can be managed locally and which should be handed over to the central team. The quality of the investigations and solutions implemented must be maintained, divergence from the standard structured approach must be monitored and the right training and coaching mechanisms must be in place and functioning well. In addition, knowledge has to be retained locally, but also fed in centrally, to help solve future problems more quickly wherever they are encountered. This model requires good logging and tracking of problems to ensure that performance can be tracked against KPIs across all divisions and the data is there to detect both local and general trends and patterns to feed into proactive investigations.

The second approach is to maintain all problem managers in a central team, in one location or across several. Each problem manager has responsibility for a business area or areas, an application set or a particular technology stack. The most senior problem managers in the group own the process and the deepest skill set, with responsibility for training and for the oversight of standards and delivering good outcomes to customers. The most senior problem managers can still be assigned to the highest priority problems and those that cross over between areas. Each problem manager can have primary responsibility for one area and secondary responsibility for another (or perhaps several others, depending on workload).

This approach provides coverage for absences and helps to balance the workload, while still ensuring that each business unit or support team mainly sees the same problem manager, allowing rapport and confidence to be built up. Having all problem managers working closely together helps to ensure that coaching and peer reviews are effective, and makes it easier to manage larger problems across organisational boundaries. It solves most of the concerns of both the centralised and decentralised models.

Effective oversight and governance is simpler and an escalation process is not required. Quality and consistency is easier to maintain and divergence from the standard approach is more readily detected. Detecting local and general trends and patterns is also easier to achieve.

How to use the second version of the federated model:

- Have a centralised team, preferably all sitting together, so that they can learn from each other and maintain high standards and a consistent, agreed approach.

- Align problem managers to individual business areas or technologies, so that they get to know the systems, people and processes.

- Have a lead problem manager to maintain the relationships, manage the delivery of the problem management service, provide the necessary reporting to management and generally be the 'face' of problem management for the area. This means that each area or business line always knows who is responsible for 'their' problems.

- A system of primary and secondary responsibility helps protect against single points of failure. By covering two or three areas, each problem manager builds up experience in several areas, to help cover absences of the primary and deal with periods of higher workload. The secondary problem manager can take up problem investigations under the coaching and supervision of the primary or lead problem manager for that business unit or technology. This increases cross-platform skills.

- Leverage this combination of expertise and familiarity with the area and its people, to make the problem managers more effective in their investigations and to ensure solutions are implemented. This leads to better results overall.

An aside: Levels of service delivery

The idea outlined in Table 5.1 is related to the common approach of classifying applications and infrastructure by their criticality, and might be useful to large organisations. It is an alternative way of assigning problems to your problem management team. To use it, you need to agree levels of service in advance for particular applications or business lines, then align your problem prioritisation structure to suit. Any problem occurring in a gold service area is assigned a higher priority than one for a silver area. See Chapter 12 for

Table 5.1 An alternative way of assigning problems

Service	Description	Target (examples)
Gold	A senior problem manager leads the investigation and drives resolution activities to completion. Must meet agreed KPIs. Breaches escalated to head of problem management.	High priority problems on critical applications or infrastructure
Silver	Junior or mid-level problem manager leads investigation and drives resolution activities to completion. Might be coached by a senior problem manager. Should meet agreed KPIs as much as possible. Breaches monitored and escalated to problem management and support team leaders.	Medium priority problems on tier 2 applications or infrastructure
Bronze	A strict framework for investigation activities and resolution tracking is carried out by a vendor organisation under a service agreement. Must meet agreed service KPIs. Breaches escalated as agreed in relevant contract.	Low priority problems on non-critical applications supported by external or internal teams

more on prioritisation. A general discussion on problem management in outsourced environments is included later in the current chapter.

Problem management in smaller organisations

In small-to-medium organisations, the challenges are a little different. The main issue is how to find budget to dedicate a resource to problem management at all. At the bigger end, where the IT organisation is more than 200 staff, many such operations have a small service management team that covers change management, release management and major incident management. There is usually a service desk as well. It should be possible to appoint at least a process owner from within the service management team who could then also function as a dedicated problem manager. I will talk more about how the different roles might be combined later in this chapter as well as the best way to use whatever problem management resources you have available.

However, many small enterprises cannot afford a separate problem management function and, in general, do not have dedicated staff for most other service management functions either. Staff multi-task and know their technology environments intimately. The application teams might run agile systems development and might also adopt, or want to adopt, a DevOps approach to support.

In organisations like this, problem management is almost certainly ad hoc, perhaps running within the agile or support team daily huddles. It is unlikely that the underlying causes of recurring incidents will emerge without some good structure around the problem management process.

Other small organisations, without dedicated problem managers, often assign problem ownership to team leaders, who are given responsibility to drive problems to closure. There are several risks with this arrangement:

- There is no formal cross-service ownership of problems and, if it is not clear where the problem causing an incident actually belongs in the organisation's responsibility matrix, problems can remain unassigned. Any interaction required between teams occurs outside structures and relies on 'dialogue' according to one organisation.

- Problems are assigned where they seem to belong, which raises the risk of duplication. Multiple incidents that are actually caused by one problem might end up being investigated as several problems by multiple teams, potentially leading to confusion, duplication of effort and additional and unnecessary work.

- A cycle of 'pass the parcel' can arise as problems are reassigned from one team to another, each in turn 'proving' it is not theirs. This often happens when attempting to diagnose or categorise problems before they are investigated. It is not confined to small organisations, of course, and represents one part of the ITIL® problem management process that has not been thought through very well. I discuss this topic in detail in Section 3, Chapter 12.

Another poor arrangement for small organisations is to combine incident management and problem management into one team or one person. Although common, it is detrimental to problem management because incidents take precedence and constantly interrupt investigation activities. This is discussed in detail later in this chapter because it applies to large organisations as well.

Ideally, one team should take on the problem management role. In most small organisations, there tends to be one group, perhaps in the infrastructure support area, that by default assumes ownership of service management. I suggest that this team should also become owners of the problem management function. It is unlikely that a dedicated resource can be allocated, so at best you will have part-time problem managers. This is where adherence to a structured model and putting people through training in problem-solving techniques pays dividends. People will not be dealing with problem management all the time, so a solid framework will make it easier for them to fall back into good habits and quickly recall the agreed approach that has been proven to give the best results previously. Consider giving problem management responsibility to the most senior person in this team to ensure it gets the right level of attention and so that you can leverage the experience and knowledge that this person will most certainly possess.

For organisations where the IT team is around 25 people, problem management is going to be a general technique shared across the senior team members. If you are in this situation, the ideas in this book are still beneficial, although it might be better to look at guidance for implementing overall service management for small enterprises. A useful book of this type is *IT Service Management for Small IT Teams* (Poppleton and Holmes, 2011) from BSI.

CASE STUDY

I have been asked many times how many problem managers are required for a given workload of problems. This is a difficult question and, honestly, I have yet to come up with a 'scientific' answer. Of course, there will never be enough problem managers to handle every problem you have, which is why you must prioritise to make best use of available resources.

One piece of work I have done was to measure the total number of problems being raised per period, look at how many were being allocated to each problem manager versus how many were being closed, and use the difference to work out whether the size of backlog was going up or down. (The actual objective was to identify which problem managers were the most effective, by measuring their throughput from allocated problems to solved problems. The attempt to work out the number of problem managers required was a by-product.) From this I made a prediction of how many problem managers would be required to maintain the backlog at a steady level.

The results were not encouraging – it looked like we needed to double the number of problem managers available. This was in a large organisation and we already had about 25 team members, so we decided quite quickly on a federated model, with an additional proposal for a managed service approach to handling lower priority problems.

My experience has shown that a well-trained problem manager can handle between three and five problems at a time in root cause investigation, plus another eight to 12 problems in resolution implementation if the problem manager is directly involved in driving both phases of the problem life cycle. This appears to be holding true in both small organisations with only a few problem managers and larger enterprises with a correspondingly larger team.

I have yet to find a way to organise problem management that allows individual problem managers to carry a higher workload, but remember that it compares quite favourably with the number of incidents that an incident manager can handle at a time – one. This contrast is a good argument for problem management as a better use of resources than dealing with a constantly high level of incidents.

To work out the size of the initial problem management team, take the number of your highest priority or severity incidents experienced in the previous 12 months and divide by 12 to give the monthly average. This number is then a rough guide to how many problem managers you will need to start. Remember, for every major incident, on average there are between five and 10 of the next highest priority. These will also need at least some problem investigation. Use this number to begin your negotiation for your initial resources.

Separation from incident management

Regardless of the organisational model you decide on, one requirement that is widely advocated is that the problem management function should be separate from incident management. The differences in the objectives between the two functions have already been covered, and they are part of the reason why it makes sense to run the problem and incident management processes in separate teams.

However, the main reason to separate the two functions is more basic: asking incident managers to do problem management in their 'spare time' always fails because they never find the time to do problem management. This means problem management takes a permanent and ineffective second priority as their focus is very correctly on incidents in progress – so it is very important that problem management responsibility is not given to incident managers.

An exception might occur when dealing with major incidents. It is quite common for problem managers to get involved in some way or even to take over when incidents are not progressing effectively. This situation is not recommended and it is easy to see that it is pointing to a skills and training issue with your incident management team more than anything else. In small organisations, there appears to be an expectation that the problem manager will step in to be the major incident manager.

From my experience, the distraction issue is very real. When I was one of two team members, sharing incident and problem management roles, only a quarter of a resource was being applied to problem management, with the other one and three quarters being consumed by major incident management.

Avoid combining incident and problem management roles – it does not work.

PEOPLE AND SKILLS

One of the reasons that some organisations try to combine the incident manager and problem manager roles in one team or one person is that the skills and attitudes are not all that different between the two, even though the processes themselves have different objectives. Both roles need a calm disposition and a structured approach.

In problem management, like incident management, analytical skills are more important than technical skills. Like a good detective, problem managers need to be methodical, evidence-driven and very structured in their approach, working carefully through the evidence to arrive at what, on the balance of probabilities, truly caused an incident or might in the future. The main skill set is always a good knowledge of problem-solving techniques.

Technical skills are an advantage, but they need to be very broad. If all you know about is networks, you might not be able to use that knowledge to find causes that relate to application coding.

Technical knowledge is useful to give the confidence to challenge SMEs, particularly if they are invoking their deep technical knowledge to suggest that their opinion should be accepted without question. Problem managers should always seek evidence to support assertions, ensure that alternatives are properly assessed and that actions proposed are sensible (and that they really have been done when people say they have been). Having said that, it is entirely possible to be an excellent problem manager with no technical skills at all.

The other key ability required of a problem manager is to be able to draw people together and be open with them. Collaboration and negotiation are skills that can be taught, but the best problem managers should have a natural inclination to want to work with other people rather than prefer to solve problems in isolation. Technical experts can work like that, but problem managers need to be able to guide and control a group to get the best outcomes. I talk more about group problem-solving below.

When recruiting or selecting problem managers, look for candidates who have been methodical and have applied a structured approach to solving problems or managing situations. They should be able to show that they are open and prefer to work collaboratively, so ask for examples of collaborative problem-solving as well.

Subject matter experts

Problem management involves more people than just the problem managers. A wide range of staff with relevant expertise get involved in investigating and resolving problems, for example:

- application developers;
- application support teams;
- infrastructure support staff;
- engineers and architects;
- application owners;
- project management staff;
- process owners.

I refer to all these people as subject matter experts (SMEs). You might see SMEs referred to as 'resolver groups' or there might be a term already in use in your organisation to mean the same thing. Use whatever term makes most sense for your enterprise. Through training, SMEs get to know how the process works, how they get involved and what is expected of them.

Vendors and suppliers are also engaged as SMEs, when appropriate. This might be through logging technical assistance calls or through contracted support arrangements.

Management and customers participate as well by agreeing and setting the priority of problems, approving resolution proposals, including spending and resource allocation, and by receiving regular updates and reports on problem investigations.

Engagement with SMEs

The fact that problem management is very dependent on SMEs introduces resource contention as a key risk to success. Problem investigations cannot progress if SMEs are not available. While there will be some priority because of the impact of the incident (remember we are starting with reactive problem management), what tends to happen is that, as soon as service is restored, people's focus turns back to what they were doing.

Your SMEs will be very busy with day-to-day support activities, servicing requests, maintaining the environment, resolving incidents and working on projects. You have to compete with these demands to get resources assigned to problems, so engaging in problem investigations needs to have a higher priority than day-to-day support. This can be a challenging message to get across. You need management support and, in particular, the team leaders of the SME groups on your side.

Simply assigning team members to problems – for example, sending them root cause analysis meeting invitations or giving them tasks and expecting their involvement – usually does not work. Quite rightly, they will focus on what their leadership wants done, not on the problem. Avoid this approach.

Often, the only way to get resources is to work through your organisation's existing resource allocation process. This could be as formal as a roster system for SMEs to be available for problem work or simply a matter of asking the team leaders to put someone on the problem.

A good way to handle less formal engagement models is to nominate a standard contact for given skill sets. Make sure that problem management has a lead SME contact or manager for each area who has the authority to allocate resources. Naturally, this is often the manager of the team, which is fine, but can it be a bottleneck if they are not available. Many teams have the idea of a 'queue manager', a rotating role whose job it is to handle the workload coming into the team or area from all sources. It could be as simple as getting SME requests added to that role's responsibility.

Engaging SMEs is an ongoing challenge that needs constant management to ensure success. Once problem management is embedded and working, resource contention becomes less of an issue, because staff understand the value and the priority of problem management. Until then, the best approach is to make sure the team leaders are the first to go through the familiarisation training. Also, schedule problem investigations immediately after service is restored, so that people are still focused. I talk more about how to do this in Chapter 6.

Another approach to engaging with SMEs is to propose that team leaders trade 10 per cent of their resource time now for three months, to get back double in return, gained from reducing the incidents their teams must respond to. I have used this idea once and it was partially successful. You need to decide if it could be useful in your situation.

Other essentials

There are a few key requirements that problem managers need in order to be effective, including meeting management, collaboration, facilitation, dealing with difficult issues and the rules of engagement.

Problem management involves running a lot of meetings, such as root cause analysis and solution development sessions and reporting or management meetings. Good meetings have a clear agenda and a chairperson to keep people on track; they get to the point quickly and are an effective use of people's time. It follows that problem managers should be equipped with effective meeting management skills and learn how to manage meetings properly.

Training in meeting management is readily available and your organisation might already offer a suitable course. If not, two resources you might find useful are *Running effective meetings by the book*, a review of 10 books on running meetings (Meeting for Results, 2013) and *How to save time and money by managing meetings effectively* (Gilbert and Smith, 2008).

Service management processes typically cut across organisational boundaries and problem management is no exception. Many organisations find cooperation between teams difficult and I have observed this first hand on many occasions. Problem management needs to be collaborative to be effective, but it can also become a driver for improved collaboration across the organisation. In one case, staff reported a marked increase in the willingness to collaborate in tasks of all types about 18 months after problem management was introduced into the enterprise.

It has been said that listening drives collaboration. Frequently at the outset and occasionally after implementation, problem managers will encounter people who are reluctant to engage in problem management. My advice is to take them for a coffee and listen to them. Seek to understand why they are resistant. Sometimes, the issue is a general reluctance to speak up, or it might be a fear of pointing fingers or being blamed for something. On one occasion it became clear that there was some discomfort that their technical skills might be questioned. Just listening can often break down the barriers.

One way of looking at the role of problem manager is as a facilitator. They must run the meeting, be a neutral observer, guide participants towards consensus, dampen down outspoken and forceful people and draw out quieter contributors. If conflict or disagreement arises, which is quite common, they must maintain a neutral posture regarding participants, avoid taking sides and stick to the issues and the evidence.

Facilitation is a skill, just like being a good negotiator or being good at problem-solving. I think it is a very teachable skill. *The Human Touch* (Thomas, Paul and Cadle, 2012) has a very good chapter on facilitation, as well as discussing many other personal skill areas that are beneficial for problem managers to develop. An article that you might find useful is *The added value of a facilitator when troubleshooting as a group* (Joosten, 2011).

Problem managers often find themselves dealing with difficult issues. In Section 1, I mentioned how some people might not want problems solved, for various reasons. Difficult issues can create rigidity and defensiveness. In these situations, it is worthwhile focusing on objective, shared goals and separating people from the problem. It can often be less threatening if participants self-disclose information. Factual verification also helps defuse defensiveness. Simply stating evidence as information, devoid of any emotive content, is effective at getting people to relax and treat issues as external and not personal.

The concept of 'rules of engagement' can go a long way towards building confidence and making people more willing to engage in problem management. Here is a set that I have used to help improve engagement:

- Assign no blame:
  - We only focus on what happened and why, then what can be done to stop it happening again.
  - We do not focus on who. In fact, we do not have 'human error' as a root cause.
- Attend problem sessions:
  - Problem-solving works best when a group of experts collaborate.
  - First get to a clear statement of the problem.
  - Gather all the facts.
  - List all possible causes.

- Suspend judgement:
  - Always keep an open mind and assume you do **not** know the cause.
  - Fit theories to facts, not the other way around.
- Make problem tasks a priority:
  - Take responsibility for your tasks.
  - Make your management aware of what you are working on.
  - Raise work conflicts to the problem manager.
  - Do not close tasks without review and approval.

Training

To develop any type of training, you need to know who needs to be trained and what they need to learn. The objectives of problem management training are twofold: improving skills and improving understanding and engagement. There are two objectives, so there are also two types of training. I call these skills training and familiarisation training. Skills training is for problem managers, while familiarisation training is for those who are not problem managers but get involved in problem investigations. There is a third group of stakeholders that includes managers, peers from other service specialties and customers. This group does not get specific training, other than your implementation launch material and ongoing stakeholder management approach.

Training is not a one-off exercise during the implementation project, it needs to be ongoing. It should be available for new joiners and should be re-run periodically for existing staff as a reminder of the standard approach. If you have an induction process, it should be included as one of the mandatory training modules for all SMEs. You could make exposure to your standard methodology a selection criterion when hiring problem managers.

Even if candidates have done your preferred course or something similar, all new problem managers should do the formal training in your adopted methodology soon after starting. This will refresh their understanding, clear away any bad habits from their previous role and ensure good alignment with the rest of the team.

Skills training

Some people are naturally good at solving problems, some are less so. However, everyone can be trained to improve their methods and broaden the scope of the techniques they have available. Skills training is initially aimed at your problem managers. In more mature implementations, where more people are expected to take up and run their own problems, the audience for skills training might widen.

The objective is to develop very highly skilled problem managers. You have two options. If you have people who are already problem managers, or are about to become problem managers, and who have at least some effective techniques and methods in place, you can select the most highly skilled, work through what they do and why it is effective and put together training materials based on that.

Secondly, if you do not have people already skilled, but have one or more people selected with the right aptitude and attitudes, you might want to consider an external course instead. Everyone who will be a problem manager should do the same course, including you. Then you build your structured approach on the same framework, so the course is directly applicable. You should also build your familiarisation training to reflect this approach as well.

> Consider either Kepner–Tregoe training from KT or KEPNERandFOURIE training from Thinking Dimensions for your problem managers. There are plenty of other training types available, but these two are the ones with which I am most familiar and feel comfortable recommending. I cover all the frameworks I have found so far in Chapter 13. Most have associated training offerings.

Once everyone is trained, backup the training with ongoing coaching from your more experienced problem managers or from training vendors. Regular quality audits and sitting in on problem investigations will help ensure that your problem managers do not drift away from the standard approach. Although I do not include a sample skills training course here, I will cover a workable structured approach to problem-solving later in this chapter.

Familiarisation training

Familiarisation training is not just for imparting knowledge about problem management, it is also a key to winning people over and making future engagement much easier.

There are two basic ideas behind how I approach familiarisation training. The first is that problem management is one of those processes that is easier to learn by doing it. There is a Vietnamese proverb, quoted in the book *The power of positive deviance* (Pascale, Sternin and Sternin, 2010, p.34), that says, 'a thousand hearings are not worth one seeing and a thousand seeings are not worth one doing'. These authors later distil this down to 'it's easier to act your way into a new way of thinking than think your way into a new way of acting' (ibid., 2010, p.38). You want to get people involved in problem management activities quickly, not spend hours going through the process in training sessions. This is why the training is short, focuses on what is in it for them and why they will want to get involved. You should then get them engaged in problem sessions soon afterwards.

Secondly it is good to set expectations in advance. You want to get people to come to their first analysis session with a pretty good idea of what is going to happen, what their role is going to be and how they will be expected to behave. Familiarisation training runs through the whole process quickly and then spends time talking through a typical root cause analysis session, concluding with the 'rules of engagement'.

I found that this saves a lot of time and argument during sessions. Problem managers do not have to spend the first half of a session explaining to any new attendees what it is all about, and why the meeting proceeds as it does.

A familiarisation training session covers in more detail the essentials already covered in the launch briefings. This includes what problem management is and what it aims to achieve, how it benefits the organisation and the SMEs themselves and both the essential process steps and the rules of engagement. It should not run for more than one to one and a half hours, leaving time for questions. I suggest that you spend no more than one third of the time on what problem management is and its benefits, so that you can take most of the time to go through the process steps and then spend as much time as possible on how a structured problem analysis session is run.

This should entail stepping through your standard analysis session agenda, explaining what each item is about and then running through the rules of engagement until everyone is clear about them, in particular the ideas that you should suspend judgement, avoid pet theories and be prepared to identify what is really going on.

Familiarisation training should be followed up with involvement in a real root cause analysis session as soon as possible, if not as an active participant, then as an observer. As I said earlier, once SMEs start to get involved and realise how simple it is to solve problems this way, they quickly become supporters and the ease of engagement increases rapidly. I have included a familiarisation training package that I have used successfully at www.bcs.org/probmgt-extras.

I suggest that you use internal practitioners – trained problem managers – not outsiders, to deliver the familiarisation training. Apart from costing a lot less, you maintain control of the content, you can deliver it any time it is needed without incurring additional fees and the problem managers get credibility from running the courses. For this approach to be successful, it is important to pick people who can deliver the training effectively, even entertainingly.

Familiarisation training should be mandatory for all SMEs. You should 'turn the tables' on them by not allowing them to be engaged in problem analysis unless they have done the training. I have found this to be very effective in driving engagement.

Benefits of training

I have found that training has proven to be one of the key success factors of problem management. Staff are more effective, a higher percentage of root causes are found and the time to find root cause is reduced. They also are better able to integrate the expertise of others engaged in investigations.

Problem management also becomes more consistent because all the problem managers are using the same highly effective methods. The built-in coaching and feedback loops help grow competency and capability across the team as well and you gain more problem managers with the skills and approach to address major problems.

MAPPING THE PROBLEM MANAGEMENT TEAM TO THE PROCESS

I want to stop and compare this case with many organisations in which the only things the problem managers do **not** do are the two key tasks.

CASE STUDY

Joe Gallagher is a colleague of mine that applied Lean thinking to the problem management organisation that I founded and he took over at a major international bank. He ran a 'day in the life' of the problem managers to identify non-value-adding activities. He found they spent a lot of time chasing tasks assigned to SMEs, arguing about who should take on which problem and producing a lot of ad hoc reporting for management. By going back to the key activities required to make problem management successful (see Chapter 1), he noted that there are only two tasks that are valuable for problem managers to do:

- finding root cause;
- finding and getting approval for a resolution.

He determined that everything else should be 'production-ised', essentially by getting somebody other than a problem manager to do it. I definitely agree with Joe on this.

Note that 'doing' and 'being accountable' are not necessarily the same thing. While Joe thought that the problem managers should stop doing a lot of things, he did not mean that that they should stop being accountable for the overall outcomes of the problem management process. More on this at the end of this chapter.

Problem managers fully engaged in problem analysis

Some organisations take an administrative approach to problem management. The problem manager focuses on tracking problem progress through the process, but is not engaged in leading investigations and applying problem-solving skills. Technical experts run their own investigations in their own way, without the direct engagement of the problem management function. In some cases, there is only one 'problem manager' for the entire organisation, a purely administrative role that produces reports or at best is handed problems once solved to track resolution efforts.

This approach does not work well because often technical and application staff are not trained in problem analysis. There cannot be a high degree of confidence that they will find the real cause and not just a symptom (or worse, something convenient and easy to blame). Also, as I explain below, there is good evidence that similarly skilled and like-minded teams are not as effective at solving problems as cross-functional teams.

From talking to some of the organisations that take what I call this 'passive' approach, it is clear to me that engaging problem managers fully in problem analysis ('active' problem management) results in much better outcomes, with lower problem recurrence rates than those taking the passive (management and tracking) approach.

One way of thinking about this issue is in terms of timing. In the last chapter, we talked about the end state of a problem management implementation, where problem management is so embedded in the organisation that everyone is their own problem manager. People know how to solve problems, they understand that the best approach is to investigate in groups (see below) and the structured approach is the natural way to go about it. Clearly, very few organisations will be able to adopt this approach as their starting point. When enterprises take the passive approach, they are really circumventing the natural implementation approach, jumping to the end state before building skills by going through the beginning stages.

You cannot jump over the developmental stages. If you expect people to investigate their own problems without going through the process of training them, modelling good practice and getting them used to the structured approach, you will make little difference to your current situation.

Similar to the above arrangement, you might also encounter an informal situation, where the incident or system 'owners' want to do their own investigation of root cause, actively excluding the problem managers (and everyone else). This approach is often disguised as a post-incident review. Incidents occur, the direct support team does some sort of investigation and only then is the problem handed over to problem management, with a 'root cause' already published.

Another attitude you will come across is that only technical 'experts' can be effective at getting to root cause. In other words, technical knowledge is more important than sophisticated problem-solving techniques. This attitude can make engagement difficult. The only way around this is to demonstrate results and teach the methods.

With problem managers available who have been trained in root cause analysis techniques, it makes sense to ensure that they lead investigations, applying the consistent approach developed for the organisation. The SMEs are still engaged and are vital to the success of the investigation and, once the cause is known, in evaluating what is the best solution for the problem.

Problem managers are highly skilled in problem-solving techniques, so should lead problem management investigations in conjunction with the technical experts, then work with SMEs to determine solutions to problems and track implementation to ensure the problem is entirely fixed. The problem management function should be responsible for reporting root cause, progress on resolution and all the metrics and KPIs related to problem management. It is also responsible for maintaining a consistent and structured approach to problem management across the entire organisation

You will encounter people who do not think that they need to learn about problem-solving because they are already good at it. The approach that I found to work well in this situation is to win them over by inviting them to contribute to improving other people's skills. Make them part of your core team and get them involved in teaching others how they do it. By agreeing with them, but asking them to consider the more junior people in their team, you help them understand the responsibility they have for developing problem-solving skills in others.

If resources are limited and the number of problem managers is small relative to the size of the organisation, consider making their primary function proactive problem management, with administration a secondary function. This will produce a much higher return than focusing on tracking the work done by others.

Problem management as a group activity

There is a solid body of evidence that problem-solving in groups is significantly more effective than individual efforts or investigations run by groups of like-minded individuals. Hong and Page (2004) demonstrated this by showing that diversity in perspective and ways of thinking lead to better outcomes than even the best problem solvers. Also, we tend to be 'good at producing convincing arguments, but we are also adept at puncturing other people's faulty reasoning (Jones, 2012, p.35).

A mix of 'insiders' and 'outsiders' is critical. Too many insiders leads to uniform thinking, while too many outsiders dampens the free exchange of ideas. A *New Scientist* article (King, 2012) talks about this idea and provides a number of references for further reading on this topic. Daniel Kahnemann also includes a chapter on the limitations of our thinking, when we ignore the 'outside' view, in *Thinking, Fast and Slow* (Kahnemann, 2012, pp.245–254). While he is talking about decision-making specifically, the disciplines of problem-solving and making decisions are closely related.

Inclusiveness and brainstorming can throw up surprising insights from people other than the recognised experts. Allowing problem investigations to be run privately by individuals or small, like-minded groups (like-thinking teams) often fails to realise benefits because these 'naïve' insights cannot arise. By encouraging diversity, you might find that you generate many more interesting ideas to help you solve problems.

Structuring analysis and follow-up sessions

We have talked about the benefits of a structured approach and how it is superior to ad hoc problem-solving. There are two approaches to setting up a structure, which both work. The first is to put together your own structured approach and the second is to base your structure on the well-defined methodology that you have selected and in which you have trained your problem managers. I have done both; however, I can now say that the second approach works somewhat better. Having said that, it will only work when all problem managers have done the training and you have written down and agreed the exact agenda you will follow.

To get you started, here is one structured approach I have implemented. It embeds the Kepner–Tregoe approach and was done at a time when I had done this training but the team had not. You can take the KT piece out and replace it with your preferred methodology at step 2.

Suggested standard agenda

1. Introduction.
2. Define a clear statement of the problem.

3. Draw up a system diagram.
4. Build the chronology of events.
5. Brainstorm possible root causes.
6. Work completed to date.
7. In and out of scope for problem investigation.
8. Investigation next steps.

The following gives a detailed commentary on the above steps.

Step 1: Introduction

There are always those who come to a root cause analysis (RCA) session reluctantly. They might not have experienced one before, they might not appreciate just what RCA is all about, they might feel that such a session is not needed because 'they already know what the cause is'. They need convincing that a RCA session is of use to them in the first place, but in reality no amount of talking or explanation will be effective, you have to experience a successful RCA session to understand how powerful it can be. The familiarisation training does not replace the introduction, they are complementary.

The session introduction tells the team what is going to happen and what they should expect, why the agenda is structured as it is and why the steps are in the order they are.

For instance, the reason step 6 is after step 5 is because the brainstorming session will be damaged if the team already know of work that has been done. This knowledge introduces assumptions and so influences ideas and focus. This is not immediately obvious to those team members who might not have done any formal RCA work before. They might think that they need to have all the facts together before investigating root cause.

Without making a speech, all the introduction seeks to do is to give people an idea of how the session will progress, what the ground rules are and what is expected of participants.

The introduction should also take time for everyone to get to know each other, probably just by going around the table (or on the call) for people to say who they are, where they work and what area of expertise they represent.

Step 2: Define a clear statement of the problem

The definition of the problem is the grounding for all of the steps that follow. The value of this process is that once the problem is clearly identified and stated, the possible solutions can be readily described and evaluated. However, very few organisations spend sufficient time on this definition.

An incomplete problem definition tends to be caused by the belief that the problem is obvious, which is the result of the false assumption that everyone perceives the same thing. There is a need to hurry up and get it fixed – a rush to find a solution. Organisations are so 'solution-oriented' that they fail to define the problem properly, focusing instead on their favourite solutions.

The following questions are used to describe the problem:

- Identity (What) – What part of the service does not function well? What went wrong? What expected outcome was incorrect?
- Location (Where) – Where does the problem occur?
- Time (When) – When did the problem start to occur? How frequently has the problem occurred?
- Size (Extent) – What is the size of the problem? How many parts are affected? What is/was the impact? Why does it matter?

There are some points to keep in mind when defining the problem:

- The investigation is based on the definition of the problem, so the definition has to state precisely which deviation(s) from the agreed service levels have occurred.
- Often, during the definition of a problem, the most probable problem cause is already assumed. Take care not to jump to conclusions that can guide the investigation in the wrong direction from the beginning.
- A problem definition that is too wide makes the problem impossible to solve. Defining the problem too narrowly limits the value of root cause analysis.
- Do not make any judgemental or value statements and include them in the definition because they might be interpreted as fact and incorrectly influence further investigation.

Once a clear statement has been agreed, write it up so it is clearly in people's minds throughout the analysis session. You will keep coming back to the problem statement throughout the investigation.

Step 3: Draw up a system diagram

This step of the process is useful to 'bring the system to life' for participants. Before the meeting, you should have already collected as much data as possible, including a complete system diagram (assuming there is one). However, asking one or a number of people to draw up on the board what they know about the system will bring everyone to the same level of understanding quickly. It might also bring out key areas to focus on and occasionally will even reveal facts about the problem that have previously not been known even to those who thought they knew the system well. On a teleconference, you might be able to share a screen or review a document instead.

Step 4: Build the chronology of events

This is about establishing time and activity relationships. A clear sequence of events can quite often reveal obvious cause and effect relationships as well as help to eliminate data or activities that are not relevant. Taking the time to review and vet the timeline thoroughly often reveals a surprising amount of information, including new evidence not previously brought forward. It is not just about the timeline of the incident either, it should also include as much history as is known about changes, previous incidents, unexplained events, first reports of performance degradation or unexpected behaviour, and related system and environmental factors – power outages, third-party connections, vendor patches and so on.

Step 5: Brainstorm possible root causes

This is about getting a list of all possible root causes that is as complete as you can make it. The key here is to keep people thinking up possible causes without trying to analyse, solve or eliminate any suggestions as you go. Keep an open mind, tell people the ground rules. For instance, 'We will take any and all suggestions however unlikely they might sound. Anyone who tries to start analysis or suggest what they think is definitely the root cause will be politely asked to stop and to stick to thinking of possible causes.'

Step 6: Work completed to date

This step is to go through any work that has already occurred, perhaps during the incident while service was being restored. It also seeks to gather in any activities that are already going ahead, perhaps in isolation, in any of the teams or by people involved. The problem manager should be firm about stopping any work that is not relevant to the problem in hand while bringing into the activity list any tasks that the team agree are relevant and should be pursued.

Step 7: In and out of scope for problem investigation

Often during these analysis sessions, things come up that are not related to the problem in hand, such as improvement suggestions, investigations not related to the problem and seeking other systems where this particular problem might have an impact. All these things need to be captured, but for problem analysis to be successful it is important that tasks and actions that are in scope for resolving the problem are clearly segregated from activities that will not lead to resolving the problem. Get agreement on this and make people understand that the out-of-scope items will not be forgotten, but will be taken up in other work streams.

Step 8: Investigation next steps

This is when you agree what steps are required. There could be more information required or you could go straight into analysis to identify likely causes out of the list of possibilities. This step could be thought of as setting up for another session or it could be a way of organising the current session if there is time to continue. Always remember that actions need to leave people going away with both commitment and clear responsibilities to do tasks and report back.

Note that although this step is very common, it is not always required. Depending on the complexity of the problem, sometimes the root cause can be satisfactorily established within a single meeting.

If the investigation requires more sessions, always schedule them as close together as possible, the next day or in a couple of days if it is agreed that certain tasks will take more than 24 hours. A common mistake to avoid is to allow the sessions to become weekly. This just adds unnecessary delay and does not maintain good momentum in the investigation, leading to dissatisfaction with progress and disillusionment with RCA as a discipline.

Set up a regular calendar entry for problem investigation sessions in your diary, perhaps one in the morning and one in the afternoon. This ensures your time is free when you need it. Set up a standard invitation list for root cause analysis sessions, including the relevant SMEs for your focus area, in a large organisation, or the usual SMEs you engage in a smaller place. You can then simply add the address list to one of your pre-booked meetings when you need to run a session. Keep track of any new people who are called on to attend who have not had the familiarisation training and schedule them in as an action for yourself from the meeting.

Lack of framework

Without structure, the time to find root cause can be extended significantly. One study by an ex-colleague of mine examined two teams, both doing problem management. One team did not mandate a structured approach and expected each problem manager to do root cause analysis as they saw fit. The other team had developed and agreed a structured approach using one of the major analysis frameworks. The difference was striking. On average, the first team found root cause in about 10 days, while the second team took less than 4 days. This is more than a 60 per cent advantage and lends strong support to the argument that a structured approach is critical to the success of problem management.

Regardless of the model, it is important to recognise that people will be doing problem management outside the framework, perhaps without even realising that this is what they are doing. Making the structured approach available to all to understand and use, as well as training people in the process and the methods, is well worth the seemingly extra effort.

In addition, be vigilant and protect your outcomes from people who are doing problem management without the framework and structure to do it well. This is especially important if all investigations by all teams are included in your measurement regime. I have this example that might serve to make this point more clearly.

CASE STUDY

An incorrect report was produced in a financial institution. It was used to assess the risk being taken in financial transactions. The data in the report came from a series of different applications. The problem manager who brought this situation to my attention was actually a client relationship manager with no formal training in problem management. He was observing the 'blame game' being played. Individuals were mainly focused on proving that the cause did not lie with them, putting the majority of their time into showing that their application was functioning correctly and producing the right results. Nobody was looking at the overall problem and looking for a cause systematically.

While it is possible that eventually this approach might have led to finding the cause, by a process of elimination, a lot of time and energy (and money) was being wasted. The manager was frustrated, but he was also part of the problem. He did not apply the appropriate structure to enable his colleagues to collaborate and work through the problem systematically. When problem management took over the investigation, it took one session to get everyone on the same page and another to show that the errors came from a combination of sources, including one that was no longer being updated and was intended for historical reference only. The solution was implemented 24 hours later.

Who runs error resolution?

Whether the problem management function owns problems throughout their life cycle or focuses on root cause analysis and lets other teams find and implement solutions depends on the organisation, as long as the process is structured correctly.

The two main approaches I have seen are for the problem manager to own problems through their life cycle or to hand over at an agreed point to another team for implementing the solution. Both approaches work, but each has its drawbacks. Maintaining ownership throughout is better for control, but takes problem managers' time away from their most valuable activities. Handing ownership over to another team makes better use of resources but breaks the life cycle into two parts and introduces a new point of complexity in the handover process.

In my experience, customers want to see a clear sense of ownership of problems. Having one problem manager own the problem throughout its life cycle, from first assignment to final closure, is usually seen as the simplest way to demonstrate the expected accountability. In addition, if problem managers are not accountable for problem resolution, who is and who makes sure that fixes are implemented and problems are closed correctly?

Accountability for problems through their life cycle should remain with the problem manager, but responsibility for different aspects can be assigned where it is most appropriate.

CASE STUDY

I mentioned Joe Gallagher's Lean project earlier. It also found that one of the two main bottlenecks in the problem management process was implementing resolutions to fix the causes of problems. Problems tended to pile up into a backlog waiting for implementation to be scheduled. Tracking error resolution is time-consuming and takes problem managers away from investigating root cause and finding solutions.

Error resolution activities should be assigned to the SMEs with the appropriate skills to implement the agreed solution, as long as the handover is clear and everyone knows how to track and report progress. Problem managers remain accountable for ensuring that fixes are implemented, but they are relieved from detailed task tracking that is better done by experienced project teams.

The remaining issue is ensuring that error resolution does not become a bottleneck behind which unresolved problems pile up. A key control is the ability to report accurately on the backlog of unresolved problems. It is essential to success and is an important way to ensure that problems get the right level of attention. The PAB and management reporting are the two mechanisms to maintain this control, and I cover these below and in Chapter 7.

Problem management in outsourced environments

If part or all of your IT services are provided through outsourcing, problem management is presented with a very specific challenge – who should be responsible for it, the outsourcer or the retained team? If it is the outsourcer, what confidence do you have in their findings and what incentive do they have to tell you what they find, particularly if it reflects badly on them, or worse, might make them liable for financial penalties? If your organisation does it, how do you ensure cooperation from the outsourcer and obtain the evidence you need to find root cause?

In a mature relationship, where trust levels are high, you can rely on the outsourcer to do the right thing. If you are not in this position, you need to take a different approach. Either way, contracts need to include the necessary clauses to ensure that problem management works properly. Outsourcing contracts is a large topic, well outside the scope of this book, but there are a couple of basic principles to keep in mind.

- The rules of engagement still apply. Assign no blame, look to find the cause and not who caused it and focus on beneficial outcomes for all parties.

- Think of problem management as one of the control functions, like audit. You would not allow the outsourcer to audit themselves. Indeed, there are probably laws and regulations against this. Similarly, your contracts will include audit rights, such that your organisation can meet its regulatory obligations. Problem management should have similar rights. Your organisation should retain the overall accountability for problem management and there should be clauses in the contract that require cooperation from the outsourcer (at their reasonable expense) in your investigations.

 Always keep the problem management function in the retained organisation and ensure that your right to investigate problems is in the contract.

When you have multiple vendors, it is a little more complicated because this is where finger-pointing reaches a new level. Patterson (2012) points out that 'during problem analysis, service providers can focus on attributing blame rather than identifying the root cause'. The solution is probably to adopt a service integration and management

(SIAM) approach. This means that the natural place to locate problem management is in the SIAM function – a team in the retained organisation. Patterson's article and white paper are a good place to start in understanding SIAM concepts.

One point to keep in mind is that you and the outsourcer are unlikely to manage services on the same tool platform. Attempting to integrate platforms so that problems and incidents can be tracked across the two organisations is expensive and complex, unless one organisation has the leverage to force the use of their toolset on the other. I advise that you do not try to integrate at the toolset level; simply ensure your processes are able to manage problems across organisation boundaries manually. Only consider tool integration if the costs can be justified in terms of significant improvement in service outcomes for the customer organisation.

GOVERNANCE AND PROBLEM ADVISORY BOARD

The PAB was developed by Dennis Adams of Dennis Adams Associates and is based on the change advisory board concept. Consisting of senior managers, the role of the PAB is to provide governance, helping to decide which problems should be investigated, allocating resources, approving resolution plans and budgets, ensuring benefits are realised and generally monitoring the problem management function. The membership of the PAB depends on the individual organisation; however, like the role that the sponsor plays in managing projects, it needs to have the authority to approve spending and allocate resources to problems and away from business-as-usual work, with the additional responsibility of deciding which problems should be investigated and which can be put aside.

There are several advantages in having such a board:

- For proactive problem management, it provides the mechanism to select which problems to investigate, as well as choose not to investigate others, due to lack of resources, insufficient return for effort, and so on.

- It allows the customers and management to be involved in choosing problems to investigate.

- It can ensure that investigations are properly resourced and funded, which is not always easy for the problem management function to achieve otherwise.

- It can provide the forum for selecting and approving spend on proposed error resolution actions.

- To a lesser extent, it can also be the forum for reporting progress on individual problem investigations, particularly for major problems.

The PAB is the ideal governance structure for the review stage of the process:

- It can accept or reject the closure of problems, depending on whether it is convinced that the problem has been fixed.

- It can give approval to move problems to the deferred state, accepting that root cause cannot be found, or that the solution proposed has been rejected for good reason and therefore the problem cannot be closed.

- It could decide instead that a problem should go back for more investigation of cause or to find a better, cheaper or more acceptable solution.

See Chapter 15 for more about the review stage of the process.

One of the most important functions of the PAB is to approve or reject resolution proposals. It is the ideal forum to make sure that error resolution works properly. The board can agree to implement or reject solutions and, if accepted, to assign resources, adjust and agree the implementation schedule and give the necessary authority to drive resolution and ensure problems really get fixed.

As a decision-making forum, minutes are always required. These can be quite simple, for example just a list of attendees and absences plus a list of the decisions made (see Figure 5.1). Minutes with actions to track from meeting to meeting are probably not required and might distract the board from its function. The minutes should be published to the management team after every PAB meeting.

Figure 5.1 PAB minutes template

Problem Advisory Board Minutes DD MMM YYYY							
Attendees	Date 1	Date 2	Date 3	Date 4	Date 5	Date 6	Date 7
Member 1	Y	N	Y	Y			
Member 2	Y	Y	Y	Y			
Etc.							
Closure requests							
Problem no.	Problem statement				Approved		Y/N
Solutions proposed							
Problem no.	Problem statement						
Costs	XX	Resources required			YY		
Target date	dd mmm yyyy				Approved		Y/N
Move to pending							
Problem no.	Problem statement						
Reason							
Follow-up date	dd mmm yyyy				Approved		Y/N

(Continued)

Figure 5.1 (Continued)

Solutions proposed				
Problem no.	Problem statement			
Proposed by	Name			
Priority assigned		P1/P2/P3	Approved	Y/N

Depending on your organisation, you might need a terms of reference and even a board charter. If so, I suggest that you be guided by your organisation's requirements.

CASE STUDY

This is how I launched a quite successful PAB:

'Beginning this Friday, a new governance body is being introduced, the problem advisory board or PAB. The PAB will consist of the IT operational management team.

The role of the PAB is to provide governance of the problem management function:

- deciding which problems should be investigated;
- setting priorities;
- allocating resources;
- approving resolution plans and budgets; and
- ensuring benefits are being realised.

The general format of the board is:

- Summarise progress and answer questions on recent major problems, including investigations and resolutions.
- Approve problems proposed for closure.
- Present proposals for new problem investigations for approval and prioritisation.
- Request assistance for any problems that are not getting the support they need, either for investigation or to drive forward with implementing fixes (resolution).
- Review volumes of problems in various states and how long they are there, to govern the process and ensure that problems are being resolved and incidents are being reduced.

The board has senior management approval to be constituted and will have full authority to make binding decisions. Invitations will follow.'

Roles and responsibilities

To wrap up this chapter, I want to return to the assignment of roles and responsibilities. Once you have worked out who gets involved in the major phases of the process, it is time to put together a roles and responsibilities matrix, often termed a RACI, for Responsible, Accountable, Consulted and Informed. I think this can be kept simple, with a focus on the major steps, the major players and how each is involved (see Table 5.2).

Table 5.2 RACI matrix (R – responsible, A – accountable, C – consulted, I – informed)

Role	Select problems	Find root cause	Find solution	Approve solution	Implement solution	Close problem
Problem manager	C	A	A	R	A	A
SMEs	C	R	R	C	R	C
PAB	A	I	I	A	I	R
Customers	C	I	I	I	C	C
Senior management	C	I	I	C	I	I

6 REALISING THE BENEFITS OF PROBLEM MANAGEMENT

This chapter focuses on the key benefits of problem management and how to realise them, and concludes with a discussion of effective communication.

To make problem management truly effective, it is important, firstly, to make sure everyone clearly understands your commitments to your customers, including how problems are prioritised and tracked. Secondly, you need to keep good records about the types of causes and to classify them into an informative structure. Thirdly, you need to make sure problems actually get fixed and all the information discovered is captured in such a way that it is available to improve services in future.

COMMITMENTS

A set of commitments for how problems will be managed is a valuable way to ensure that your team understands what is expected of them. These need to be available to all the stakeholders, including the team. As well as setting out how you will measure performance, you can detail how problems are taken up and what communication can be expected.

The rules of engagement that you share with your SMEs should also be made available to everyone. While the rules themselves are more specifically about SME engagement and usually explained verbally in your familiarisation training, publishing your commitments allows you to set out the reasons behind them.

You should also include other points, such as committing to log everything in order to make sure problems do not get 'lost' or giving clear reasons why a problem might not be taken up. It is also useful to commit to prioritising according to a set of rules, while giving stakeholders the opportunity to have their say in which problems should be investigated first.

Below is a set of commitments I have used before. They include the targets agreed for managing problems and cooperation between problem managers and their colleagues and vendor partners.

We need to do the following to make sure that we all realise the benefits of effective problem management.

- We will meet our operational level agreement for major problems:
  - Problem investigation will commence within 24 hours of service restoration.
  - First progress report published within 24 hours and regularly after that.
  - Root cause will be found within five working days in 80 per cent of cases.
  - Solutions will be implemented in the agreed time-frames in 90 per cent of cases.
  - If we cannot find the cause or we cannot fix it, we do not close the problem; it is deferred and tracked separately until it can be solved.
  - We will report how our performance measures up against our KPIs.
- We will be fully collaborative:
  - Problem management works best when people work together to solve problems, so we commit to always investigate as a group.
  - Priority will be agreed jointly and not set solely by the problem manager.
  - We will encourage a collaborative environment and help it to spill over into how teams interact in other situations.
- We will assign no blame.
  - Problem management is about finding the real cause and fixing it so it cannot happen again. It is not about allocating blame to individuals or teams and we will never assign blame when we report causes.
  - We will help people to understand that we are not assigning blame, to make it much easier to get to real causes and to improve engagement.

CLASSIFICATION AND ROOT CAUSE CODE STRUCTURES

Another key factor for success is your classification system for root causes. A good root cause analysis process and a good method for classifying the root causes found contribute to the reduction in incidents because they provide data for analysis to uncover future problems before they can cause future incidents. I covered finding root causes in Chapter 5 and I will talk about the related subject of categorising problems in Chapter 12.

A systematic way of capturing root causes as a set of codes is essential to good analysis. Let me give an example to clarify, by contrasting two sets of cause codes (see Table 6.1). Set one is a real set I have seen, set two is just for illustration.

Looking at the two different classifications shows that team one does not have enough information to know what exactly is wrong because there are so many human errors. In contrast, team two has much more specific information available that lets them target proactive problems – for example to investigate why failover is frequently not available.

Table 6.1 Two sets of cause codes

Set one (team one)	Problems	Set two (team two)	Problems
Hardware	4	Application processing error	4
Human error	7	Failover not available	7
Not found	3	Lack of testing	3
Process	2	Patching not up to date	2
Software	6	Process not followed	6
Vendor	3	Vendor in breach of contract	3
	25		25

Not enough info | *Better, allow further questions as to why so many xxx probs*

I think you can see what I am trying to say. Effective classification of causes leads to better outcomes more rapidly. Realising early benefits can easily be constrained by poorly thought out root cause codes or no cause codes at all. These illustrations are single-level structures, but in order to be able to categorise as many circumstances as possible, it is best to create a hierarchy, which simply means a set of codes that are organised in layers of category and subcategory. Many tools support subcategories, with some going down to three and four levels.

For example, the single layer code 'application processing error' might be represented as 'application' at level one, with 'processing error', 'data validation error', 'memory exception' and so on at level two to represent the types of application problems you might find. Another level one code, such as 'batch processing', could share these level two codes, as well as having extra ones available, such as 'input file not available'.

Some careful consideration of first, second and third or fourth level codes will deliver a comprehensive method for showing not only where the cause is located, but also detail the cause – for example 'application – processing error – release – testing'.

> To make a hierarchical structure work, it is essential that searches can be performed at all levels. As well as being able to show all the problems with causes related to 'application' and 'processing error', it should be possible to extract all problems related to 'processing error', categorised by all the higher levels ('application', 'batch') that include processing errors, as well as all the lower level causes.

As always, the best way to come up with a method for organising your data is to start from the questions that need to be asked. These might include, for example, 'How many problems are caused by bad changes related to implementation as opposed to faulty planning?' or 'What types of problems are impacting applications or infrastructure elements with high volumes of incidents?' A senior colleague of mine, Joe Gallagher, expanded on this approach in a blog post from 2012:

> I like the two levels 'Where' and two levels 'What' structure. It allows us to look at trends from the top down (how many application-related root causes we have? How many external service provider root causes we have?), bottom-up (how many manual errors occurred? How many capacity issues?) and a combination of both (how many Unix Server problems were related to CPU failures? How many applications problems were due to date logic code defects?) (Gallagher, 2012).

In addition to having root cause codes structures, problem records should also have a description field to state the root cause in words. This additional information is very useful for reporting and for developing codes further.

When setting up a classification system, you do not need to cover every eventuality. You just need enough codes to cover the majority of causes and then add in an 'other' category to catch things that do not fit. The key factor in having an 'other' category is to regularly run reports to see what types of causes are being found that do not fit your hierarchy. Use the description field to help decide what additional categories would be useful. You should only add new codes with the agreement of the PAB or similar governing body.

If you add a code, update the problems that led you to this new code by replacing 'other' with the new code. This improves your data for future analysis.

The configuration system is another source of information about where problems are located. All problems should record the configuration item that was the source of the cause. By correlating the configuration item with the cause codes, you can generate powerful analyses of the sources of problems. In addition to finding general problems relating to 'application releases where processing errors were introduced because testing was inadequate', you can also be very specific about which applications have this type of problem. This might be very useful information to take back to the relevant teams and customers, in order to implement improvements in standards, training or their approach to testing releases.

Change as a root cause

An often-quoted statistic is that between 40 to 80 per cent of incidents are caused by change. This information is actually not very useful; it simply points to poor categorisation of problems by cause. Change management is the pipe through which new or updated elements get into the production environment, and it is usually these elements that cause the problem, not the change itself. Therefore, reporting a root cause as a 'failed change' is not very useful, nor is it a proper root cause.

The obvious question that will lead to root cause is 'why did the change fail?' Of course, there might be instances when the change process itself is the cause, for example, doing an unapproved change or a change that was forced through (perhaps by senior management) without proper risk assessment and testing.

There is a common belief that no change means no incidents – certainly a change freeze will reduce incidents in an immature organisation. However, changes done well should not lead to incidents. Problem management can help to improve the change process by getting to the real root cause of failed changes.

Human error as a root cause

Many problem management toolsets I have seen have 'human error' in their default list of error or cause codes. Several problem management implementations I have seen allow the use of this cause. Reviewing many discussions about root cause on major forums shows that human error is widely accepted as a valid root cause. However, it should not be.

A carefully argued criticism of human error as a valid cause is by Sidney Dekker, a professor in the field of system safety, in his book *The Field Guide to Understanding Human Error*. He says that 'human errors are symptoms of deeper trouble ... the starting point of an investigation' (Dekker, 2006, p.18). The simple test I use is 'why did the human error occur?' There is always an answer, which indicates that you have not found cause yet; you still have further to go in your investigation.

Dekker also highlights the connection between assigning blame and thinking human error is a valid cause (2006, pp.9–10). Assigning blame is actually bad problem management because it fails to get to the real cause and discourages people from revealing mistakes. Managers and system owners are particularly prone to blaming others, to deflect attention from themselves or from the system that they designed or manage. Not allowing human error as a root cause is the other half of the logic of including 'assign no blame' in the rules of engagement for problem management.

One cause or multiple causes?

An issue that frequently arises is the debate about whether a problem can have only a single root cause or several? There are two schools of thought.

- Each problem always has one cause that, if fixed, will stop that problem ever happening again.

- Problems can be caused by a combination of events working together and all these causes need to be addressed to prevent the problem recurring.

Both views have adherents who sometimes engage in heated debate. For the practical problem manager, it probably does not matter, provided you can agree which approach will be adopted and how the different situations that might occur should be handled.

One cause is all that is supported by most toolsets without modification, so it is simplest to take the one cause approach. Establishing one cause also makes the problem-solving process more straightforward. There are a few weaknesses in this approach, however. It is not always possible to agree what the exact root cause is. This can extend problem investigations unnecessarily as people attempt to determine the one true cause. There is also the danger of settling on a cause that is really a contributing factor or the trigger for the incident, not the actual root cause.

This discussion about single or multiple causes is unrelated to a practice common to several structured methodologies, where defining the problem starts by identifying one thing with one fault. This is not about having a single cause, it is about ensuring that you are investigating a clearly defined problem. One thing with one fault helps to segregate problems into specific items and greatly simplifies investigation because trying to investigate a situation that is actually two or more problems is very difficult.

In most situations, even when there is only one root cause, there tend to be contributing factors as well. Contributing factors can be identified as those factors that do not cause the problem themselves, but either create the environment for a problem to occur or increase the likelihood of a problem causing an incident. Another way of looking at contributing factors is as failure modes, from the failure mode and effects analysis (FMEA) methodology. Failure modes are usually identified individually and solutions or workarounds found for each one. This points to a method for handling contributing factors as well: handle each one individually, perhaps as tasks in one problem record, perhaps as individual problems.

CASE STUDY

Sometimes it becomes clear that an incident can only occur when two specific conditions exist. Which one is the root cause can lead to lengthy debate. For example, an incident occurred where an application received a message in an invalid format and the error handling was not adequate to deal with it. The incorrect format occurred because the customer service team routinely processed transfer requests by cutting and pasting the details of the transfer from one screen to another. This resulted in extra formatting characters being put into the field that the application could not handle and transfer processing stopped. What was the cause? While it is clear that the lack of good error handling was the root cause, the way the customer service team processed the transfers was a contributing factor. In fact, the application team were convinced that the error handling was not the cause. They viewed this as unnecessary because these characters could never get into the field and that the customer service team should be prevented from using cut and paste to prevent further errors.

The problem needed to handle both the contributing factor (please do not cut and paste into this field, it causes errors) and the lack of error handling (if this error occurs, put the transaction into a special queue for manual attention and carry on processing). It was not a very satisfactory problem to manage, neither outcome was optimal and the best solution never arose (send the transfer details direct to the message queue from the transfer request screen without any manual processing and check for valid formatting before sending).

It can be difficult to track multiple causes and resolutions in many of the available tools. If there is only one root cause field available, you have to spawn multiple related problems to manage contributing or dependent causes. You then have the challenge of how to relate all the problem records together into a coherent whole. It might be better to keep everything in one problem and, if the toolset supports it, use a subtask for each contributing factor or dependent cause. Only the primary cause is shown as the root cause of the overall problem. Tools that support multiple causes and contributing factors would be an advantage.

Sometimes, raising multiple problems is the right approach. During problem investigations, issues can be found that might not be directly related to the current problem, but should be addressed. A separate proactive problem should be raised to cover such issues that arise during the investigation of reactive problems.

What to do when no cause can be found

My least favourite feature of problem management toolsets is the ability to record 'Closed – root cause not found' in a problem record. Closing problems without finding or resolving a cause is very poor risk management practice because it simply hides the problem from view.

Do not close problems unless they are solved, which means that a cause has been found and verified and a solution has been developed and implemented. If a cause cannot be found or a solution cannot or will not be implemented, the problem record should be put into a deferred state until the problem can be solved or eliminated from the environment in some other way. See Chapter 15 for more details around managing deferred problems.

FIX THE PROBLEM

At the risk of stating the obvious, there is little point knowing what caused a problem if you do not fix it. I discussed responsibility for implementing solutions in Chapter 5. It is important to have a mechanism in place to ensure that solutions are agreed, prioritised effectively and then actually implemented. There are several reasons why this can be challenging.

Resolver groups (those who are responsible for finding and implementing the fix) might have other priorities. Incentives structures, pressure or simply the satisfaction of the work might encourage them to focus more on other tasks to meet customer demand, such as new development work.

There will certainly be limited time, budget and human resources available to deliver every requested piece of work.

An incentive to commit to solutions is to prove that problems are really the cause of incidents. Making a clear link between incidents and their cause helps to provide the necessary support for proposals to implement suitable fixes. Tracking the results of the fix in order to show real improvements in service helps to build support for the problem management process over time.

Another driver to ensure that there is sufficient focus on implementing solutions is to report regularly on outstanding tasks, including the number of problems fully resolved versus the number waiting to be corrected. Highlighting the backlog of outstanding fixes, linked to the incidents that those fixes would prevent, can be a powerful motivator of resolver team behaviour.

If you have one implemented, I suggest that the PAB should be the mechanism to ensure that solutions are approved, prioritised, funded and implemented. Good preparation by the responsible problem managers, including working with the resolver groups in advance on how a solution is to be carried out, should ensure that this is a smooth process. This might be as a specially funded project, included as a task in an existing project or the general maintenance 'book of work', or included in a future release.

Keep a record of how problems are solved, so that they are available in future to see if they could be applied again to fix other problems. This is what the Kepner–Tregoe method calls 'extend the fix'.

Consider using problem solution records to build up a record of success. It could be a separate register of major problems resolved, or simply a query set up in your knowledge base to extract a summary of problems closed successfully over a given period.

When resolution cannot be achieved

The same golden rule applies when resolution cannot be achieved as when root cause cannot be found. The problem is deferred and tracked. Again, see Chapter 15 for more details.

Larger problems

It is always challenging to decide where problem management stops and other processes such as CSI and improvement programmes in general start, particularly when dealing with what looks like a large problem. The relationship between proactive problem management and CSI is discussed briefly in *ITIL Service Operation* (Cabinet Office, 2011, p.107).

The decision to hand a problem over to CSI or have problem management do the investigation really depends on how your CSI function is defined, organised, staffed and funded. In many organisations, CSI is more of an idea and a process than a team. In these cases, problem management probably manages the work and also updates whatever CSI register there is. Where CSI is a separate team, you might hand the problem over to them. The issue then becomes who tracks it and how.

When the solution to a problem turns out to be a major project, the challenge is how problem management keeps track of the outcome to ensure that the problem is eventually resolved. In general the same parameters as for who runs error resolution apply. The problem manager is accountable and should track the project to completion, perhaps by including the due date and milestones of the project in the problem record and scheduling regular follow-up dates to check progress.

MAKE RESULTS AVAILABLE FOR FUTURE USE

Chapter 1 introduced the importance of maintaining information about problems in a format that is useful for the future and readily accessible. Knowledge flows have been recognised as a key differentiator of organisational performance (Hagel, Brown and Davidson, 2009). Sharing knowledge within and between parts of an organisation improves positive outcomes and reduces negative ones. In my opinion, this means that it follows that finding out causes and telling people is one of the value propositions of problem management.

There are two aspects to this. The first is capturing information about the types of problems being encountered, for future analysis and proactive problem management (see the discussion above about root cause codes). The second is making key information available to solve future problems or to make lasting improvements to IT services. This information includes root causes, incident symptoms, workarounds, problem solutions, incurred costs and any lessons learned or information obtained during the investigation.

This information should be readily accessible and this means that it must be searchable and recoverable through the knowledge management system. ITIL® uses 'known error' to describe this combination of information about the workaround, the root causes and the permanent fix (also known as resolution or solution). I have read many blog and discussion forum posts that demonstrate that this term is one that causes a lot of confusion.

A 'known error' is information entered into a database. It is not a step in the problem management workflow. In some tools, you will find 'known error' used as the name of the state that a problem reaches once the cause is found. I think this reinforces the confusion and I prefer to call this stage 'resolution' or 'error resolution'.

There is a natural human tendency to cover up when things go wrong, which sometimes makes it difficult to share cause information. Cultural aspects play a part as well. I have found that the key is to find a neutral, no-blame way of raising issues and publishing causes. You often have to word root cause statements very carefully and discuss them with stakeholders before publishing them.

To know that problem management is actually reducing incidents, you need to be able to connect the types of incidents occurring to their underlying causes. My method for doing this is to use knowledge management to link incidents and problems together in order to record and share information between them. In this way, information is recorded once, but remains visible regardless of whether the entry point into the data is through the service desk, the incident process or problem management.

Do not try to classify incidents by cause because until you do the problem investigation you do not really know the cause. Many incident 'causes' turn out to be incorrect after the problem investigation has completed. Several years ago, my team analysed a large sample of incidents and found that the correct cause had been recorded in only about one third of cases. The rest turned out to be 'best guesses' that were far from accurate.

Incidents are best classified by the symptoms they exhibit, not their causes. That way, first line support staff can find references to them easily when they search because customers report incidents by the symptoms they see, for example 'I cannot print', not what they think the cause might be. If you categorise incidents by cause, your service desk staff might not be able to find them again.

Relationship between incident, problem and knowledge management

I have drawn what I call a spaghetti diagram to help explain how the relationships between incident, problem and knowledge management can work (Figure 6.1). The essential idea is that the known error is a knowledge article that contains information about causes, any workarounds that were used to recover from incidents, the resolution that was implemented and other information such as any lessons learned along the way.

On the left-hand side of the diagram, I represent a simplified example of a typical incident workflow. Similarly, the basic progression of a problem is shown on the right. In the middle is the knowledge base. Both the incident record or records and the problem link to the same knowledge article in the knowledge base, which represents the known error.

1. Starting with an incident, a workaround found to restore service is recorded and a knowledge article is automatically created to retain that information. At this point, this 'known error' record is named for the symptoms shown when the incident is reported.

2. Instead of a workaround, or in addition to it, a solution might have been found to restore service. This information then either creates the known error record (because there was no workaround recorded previously) or is added to the record if it already exists. The incident investigation might also note a triggering or technical cause (see Chapter 1), and perhaps this should also be recorded.

   At this stage the knowledge article is only linked to the incident record. If a problem is raised to investigate the underlying cause of the incident, it is linked to the incident record and also to the knowledge article. The problem record will then show the 'known error' information recorded in the knowledge article as well.

3. When the problem investigation finds the root cause, this too is captured in the knowledge article as the root cause description. It is important to differentiate the root cause found in the problem from the technical cause noted in the incident investigation.

Figure 6.1 The relationship between incident, problem and knowledge management

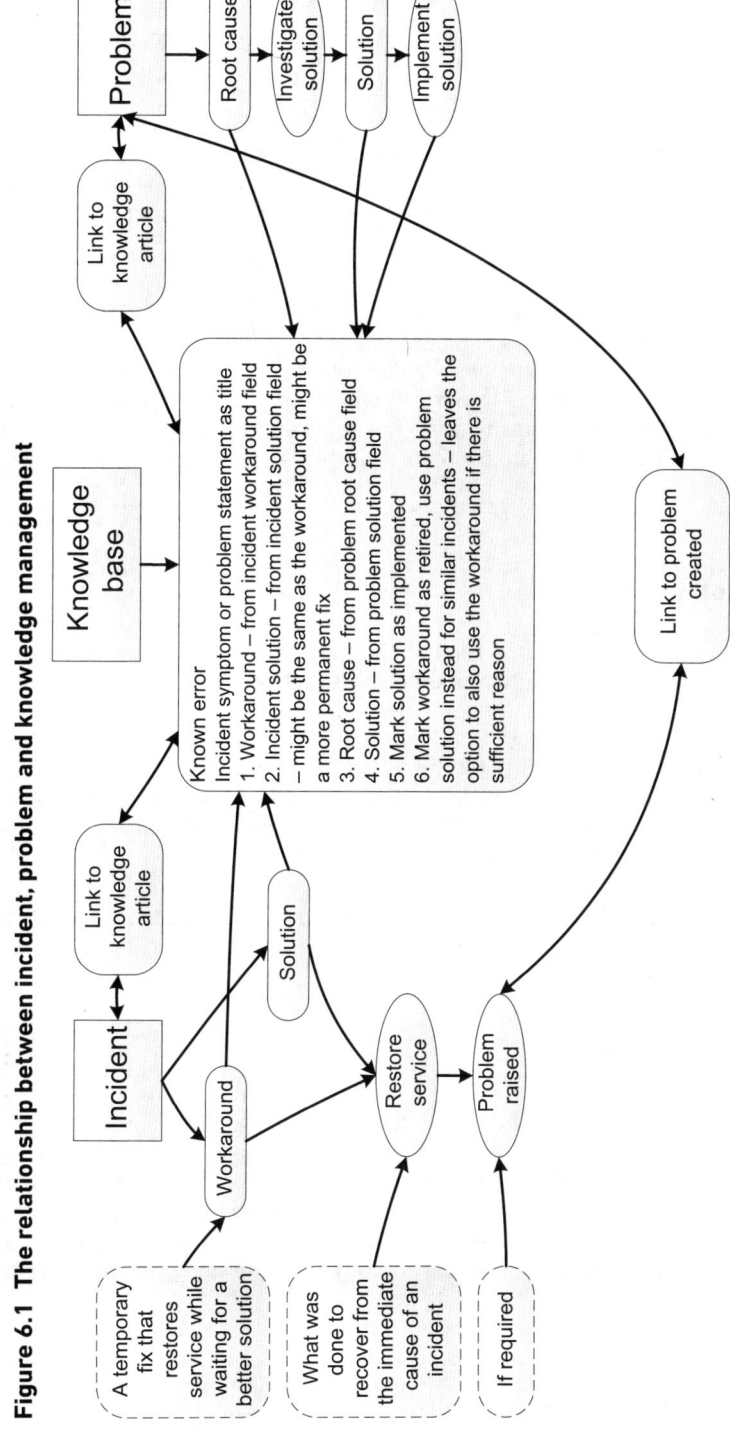

4.   The problem investigation proceeds and a solution that will fix the service permanently is found. This also goes into the known error record.

5.   When the solution is implemented, the record is updated to show that the solution is now in production.

I find this approach simple and straightforward, although not easy to implement. Tools do not typically support this approach and a manual process can be hit and miss. It is a worthwhile evaluation point, when selecting a tool, to see if it allows these relationships to be made. It should also be possible to modify an existing toolset to support it.

It is good practice to have a process or protocol in place to mark a workaround as 'retired', 'inactive' or 'superseded', once a permanent fix is in place. If a related or similar incident occurs, then the permanent fix should be considered for that case, rather than the workaround. This is important when the workaround is manual, time-consuming or otherwise sub-optimal. The workaround is retained in the database as well, just in case it is a better fit for a particular situation. This is shown as 6 in Figure 6.1.

Integration with other processes

Rather than go into a lot of detail about relationships between problem management and other processes, I want to highlight one other perspective on known errors that is mentioned in the *ITIL Service Operation* book. There is a recommendation that known faults contained in new releases should be logged in the knowledge base as known errors (Cabinet Office, 2011, p.101). I think this is an excellent idea that I have never seen implemented, nor have I noticed any discussion of it in the various forums devoted to problem management. Perhaps organisations need to reach a high state of maturity before this is seen as a natural thing to do?

I mention it here because it has a lot of merit and could form part of the handover process between development and operations, regardless of the application development process in place.

EFFECTIVE COMMUNICATION

There is a lot of material available about how to engage in effective communication and I am confident that I cannot cover the subject any better here. It is as much about listening as it is about pushing out information. I wrote about the communication plan for the implementation in Chapter 4, so here I simply want to cover a few points about the need to use the communication channels already in place in your organisation and to get into a detailed discussion of what to communicate when in the problem management life cycle.

For those who want a briefing in good communication practices, I can readily recommend the chapters relating to communication in *The Human Touch* (Thomas, Paul and Cadle, 2012). In particular, its Chapter 7 summarises the communication process neatly.

Existing organisational approach to communicating

Most IT organisations have a preferred method for talking to their customers and business stakeholders. Problem management will be more successful if it fits into the existing arrangements. The ownership of relationships and communication to customers will probably already be decided, so communicating about problems will mainly be about providing concise and clear information that other people can use to send the appropriate messages to their audience.

At least at the beginning, problem management is an internally facing process. It is usually best to feed into the existing relationship management process rather than expect to be communicating directly. Problem management does not need to face outwards because it is focused on overall service improvement. Recognition comes from IT management through the results being achieved and reported internally.

Publishing updates and the results of investigations publicly might be troublesome. Some people might not feel that the content suits being communicated to customers or business management. The message could be seen as being too blunt or perhaps not needing to be said, particularly if it portrays IT unfavourably (if the cause was that someone made a mistake, for instance). However, a quick survey I ran at a 2010 seminar of problem managers showed that most believe that customers (even paying customers of an outsourcer) prefer to know exactly what is happening. The best solution might depend on your own organisational culture, which might be something that is part of a wider organisational change. As time goes on and as trust is built, you might find yourself partnering more with client service and IT service managers to deliver concise information directly.

Communicating about problems

Communication from within the process itself, through the life cycle of individual problems, needs structure to be effective. It also needs to meet different needs at different stages. I regularly hear of criticism from IT's customers that they do not know what IT is doing to address issues that are causing interruptions to business services. They experience an incident, service is restored and (hopefully) they are told that it is fixed and then... nothing. Addressing this concern is the primary objective of the problem management communication process.

I use Figure 6.2 as a training aid when I talk about reactive problem management and the life cycle from the occurrence of an incident through to the implementation of a fix for the root cause. I readily admit that it looks a little complex, but it is actually quite straightforward once explained.

Reading from top to bottom, the diagram represents the process flow from the occurrence of an incident through to its resolution and the restoration of the service, then the handover to the problem management process and the progress through the problem process until a solution is finally implemented to address the cause of the incident permanently.

From left to right, there is first a representation of the customer perspective, then boxes showing the steps of the process, then the timeline in the centre. On the right, the regular status updates are shown, then the more formal reporting requirements and when they should occur and, on the far right, the interaction with the known error record in the knowledge base. I covered the interaction with knowledge management earlier in this chapter.

Let me start with the customer perspective on the left-hand side. How incidents and problems are handled impacts directly on the perception of the service offered by an IT organisation, and the critical success factor is effective communication. One of the first things people often ask after an incident is 'What caused it?' When people demand a 'cause' in a very short time-frame, what they are really asking is 'How exposed are we to another occurrence? Will this happen again? How is it being managed?' They are asking about the risk to their business.

Reporting a cause quickly is a common response and you will often hear incident managers telling customers what they think is the cause. Most toolsets include a cause field, which reinforces this behaviour. Remember, this is before root cause analysis has taken place, so at this point, the actual cause is not usually known, although there are situations when the real cause is discovered in the course of resolving the incident.

Stating a cause here might be well intended, but it also leads the customer to assume that the issue has been fixed.

It is better for incident management to answer the real questions and tell customers that the cause is being investigated (by problem management) and list all the steps that have been put in place to mitigate the risk of a recurrence and minimise the impact should it recur while the cause is being investigated. This 'gap' between the incident being handed over and the problem manager reporting the cause, which naturally takes time to find, can be covered by issuing an incident report that states:

- the basic facts of the incident (duration, business impact, any ongoing effects, how it was resolved);
- what preventative measure or workaround is in place;
- what additional monitoring or alerting has been implemented;
- who is on standby to respond to a recurrence;
- the symptoms to watch out for; and
- that the incident has been handed over to problem management for root cause analysis.

This is the intention of the incident report shown at the top of the second column of boxes from the right. Problem management then continues to provide daily (if necessary) status reports until a cause is found. Then you can report weekly on the resolution approach and progress until the fix is in place. Finally you can report that the problem has been closed and will not recur.

Figure 6.2 The incident/problem life cycle

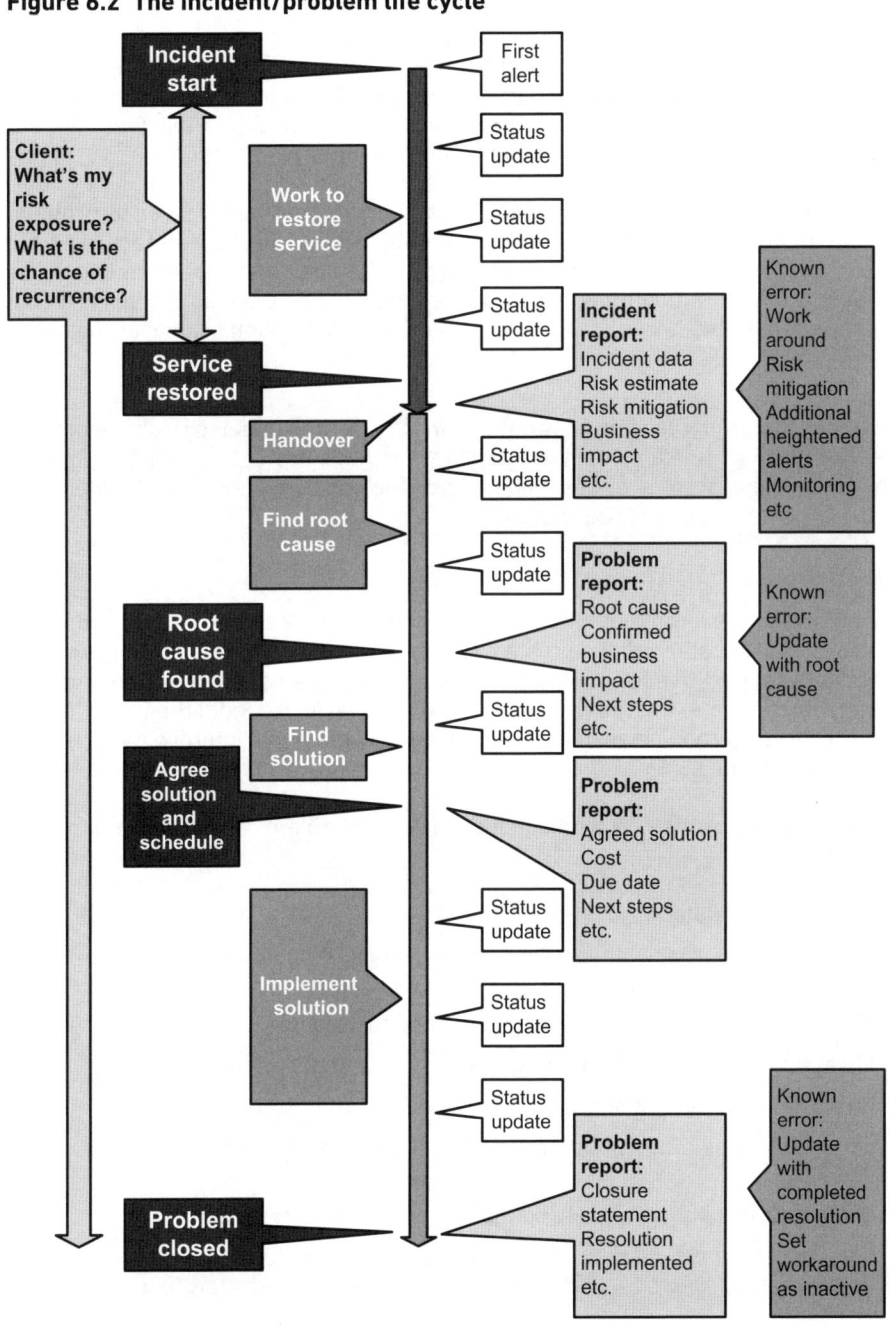

This approach works because the customer really only wants reassurance that effort is going into solving the problem and that the risk is being managed effectively. In this way you keep the customer engaged and avoid the false sense of security from reporting an assumed cause, which might or might not be correct. It only takes a few episodes to change expectations completely, although it can be hard to stop incident management or a client services team falling back to reporting the 'cause' and following the old behaviour. It needs patience and education to embed the new approach.

Once a problem has been raised and incident management hands over to problem management, it is essential to continue to communicate, so that customers maintain a sense of progress and confidence in the service. Regular status reports should be short but informative. I recommend a structured email, simple enough to be read on a smartphone. If possible, these status reports should be generated from your toolset.

Remember that, depending on your organisation, reporting updates might be going to service or client relationship managers, who might simply take the information and include it in a larger overall service report. The easier it is to copy the data, the better – another reason why simple text works best.

Figure 6.3 gives an example of what these reports can look like. This is a template I have used to extract data from the problem record to generate an emailed status report. Many toolsets support this functionality. As the content relies on fields entered in your problem record, once extracted, the email should be reviewed, edited and any typing errors or technical jargon cleaned up. Over time, the content will improve and the need for editing will diminish.

Here is a summary of the communications, once the problem team has taken up the investigation.

- First problem update:
  - The first status report should be sent less than 12 hours after handover to problem management.
  - The medium should be a formatted email status report.
  - Always name the problem manager and the investigation team members.
  - Give a clear statement of the problem.
  - Show the status of the problem, which is likely to be 'root cause analysis' at this stage.
  - Set out what is known so far and the current lines of investigation.
  - Note what the next steps will be and when the next update will be sent.

Figure 6.3 Problem report template

From: <Problem management team mailbox>

To: <standard problem communications address list>

CC: <problem investigation team> (SMEs involved in the investigation should always know what is being reported)

Email title: Problem <problem number> <problem statement>

Report body:

Problem <Problem Number>

Problem Statement: <'Short Description' goes here>

Problem Summary: <'Description' goes here> more details about the problem

Investigates: <'Incident Number 1', 'Incident Number 2', etc.> (or 'Proactive' if not incident related)

Status: <Investigation/Root Cause cannot be established/Root Cause confirmed/ Assess and Propose Resolution/Resolution in Progress/Closed> from the status field of the problem record, depending on the stage in the process

Problem Manager: <'Assigned To' goes here>

Root Cause description: <Insert contents of 'Root cause description' field> or <'Investigation in progress'> if root cause not yet found

<Investigation progress:> / <Resolution progress:> (depending on problem state)

Summary of activities, including Problem meeting was held xx/xx at xx AM PM

(There should be a field in the problem record that is specifically intended to capture updates intended for reporting)

<Next steps:>/<Additional Information:> <delete if no additional information or next steps>

Please contact the problem manager for any questions or clarifications

- Regular problem updates:
  - In the investigation stage, publish updates every 24 hours. This is normally sufficient to meet expectations.
  - The medium should be a formatted email status report.
  - Give the current status of the investigation including a list of all possible causes.
  - Show any possible causes that have been eliminated.
  - Provide an update on the progress of investigation activities.

- Note what the next steps will be and when the next update will be sent.
- Repeat regular updates until cause is found or it is decided that it cannot be found.

- Root cause statement:
  - Publish the root cause as soon as it is found or, if it is decided that it will not be found, announce 'root cause not found'.
  - The medium should be a formatted email status report; however, depending on the organisation, a formal report might be required as well, based on the content of the generated report. There might be audit and regulatory requirements, or a specific customer agreement to satisfy.
  - Ensure the root cause is clear and unambiguous. If there are political or other sensitivities, take care to ensure that the wording has been reviewed with stakeholders.
  - Identify any contributing factors or related problems, as well as any proactive problems that might have been raised during the investigation.
  - Show the status of the problem, which is likely to be 'error resolution', 'solution investigation' or 'Review – root cause not found'.

- Resolution proposal:
  - Provide updates on progress in finding and evaluating possible solutions.
  - The medium should be a formatted email status report.
  - List potential solutions.
  - If a solution has been costed and resource estimates are ready, prepare a solution proposal in a suitable format for the PAB or similar governing body.

- Error resolution progress reporting:
  - Once implementation of the solution has commenced, produce regular progress reports.
  - For longer programmes of work, status updates at the PAB might be more effective than emailed status reports.
  - Reporting frequency should be adjusted to suit the timeline of the implementation. If it is a small task with a short time-frame, then a report might only be required when the tasks are complete. For larger implementations, weekly or monthly progress reports might be required.
  - Any issues, date changes or missed deadlines should be included in reporting for escalation. Again, the PAB is probably the best forum for this.

- Final closure statement:
  - Once a solution has been applied and verified, the problem should be proposed for closure to the PAB. When approved, a final report should be prepared.
  - The medium should be a formatted email status report. In addition, consider adding recently closed problems to regular management reports, news bulletins and, if necessary, a formal report might be required for regulatory or contractual compliance.

- Clearly state what the original problem was, what cause was found and what solution was implemented. It is worth reminding people of the business impact of the incidents caused or the potential incidents addressed by a proactive problem.

- Highlight any additional benefits, such as improvements to production stability.

Remember that throughout this process, the knowledge article that contains the known error information is also updated. Formal reports and emailed status reports contain valuable information that is not rapidly accessible or easily searchable when required by service desk and incident management teams.

7 METRICS, KEY PERFORMANCE INDICATORS AND REPORTING

INTRODUCTION

Metrics, key performance indicators (KPIs) and reporting on problem management is a subject that I find is not well understood. There is a wealth of material published on the subject, but I do not think much of it is very satisfactory. Many improvements can be made to the advice given on what to measure, what constitutes a good measurement, which ones are relevant to which objective and how to align the reporting of measurement to the requirements of your audience.

KPIs versus operational metrics

Firstly, what is a key performance indicator, or KPI? Many people seem to misunderstand and so see nothing wrong with reporting a 'KPI' such as 'the number of problems opened per month', when it is only a number, a statement of events and not a KPI. A simple way to understand KPIs is to rearrange the words. A KPI should indicate something key about the performance of the process, therefore the measurement should be giving you an important message about how well the process is delivering on its stated objectives.

Definitions vary about metrics and KPIs. The distinction used in this book is that metrics, specifically operational metrics, are about the internal workings of a process. They measure health and performance at the detail level, tracking the workings of the process to make sure it is functioning properly. For example, the volume of problem investigations in progress, sorted by their priority. On the other hand, KPIs are aimed at measuring success and progress, showing whether the process is developing as expected and achieving the intended objectives or not.

I contrast KPIs versus operational metrics like this:

- KPIs tell us whether we are being successful – are we hitting our targets?
- Operational metrics tell us how our process is operating – are we keeping up with the workload or falling behind? How good is the quality of our results? Are we consistent across all the problems investigated and among all our problem managers?

Management and customers are primarily interested in results, findings that improve the service. This means that they are mainly interested in KPIs because these show success in delivering results. Metrics that report the health of the internal processes are also important, although their audience is more likely to be management, not customers.

Other measurements show you what problem management is finding out about your environment. For example, what are the top five root causes per region or technology stack? What business areas are experiencing the biggest impact from unresolved problems? For want of a better term, I call these analytical metrics, which feed into proactive problem management to improve services.

Metrics drive behaviour

It is very important to understand that measurement drives behaviour. People aim for the targets they are given and, unfortunately, outcomes can sometimes be quite different from what was intended and can lead to unexpected and undesirable outcomes. Some examples might help to clarify this point.

What happens if you set a target for the number of major incidents per year? With the intention to help people focus on stability and reducing incidents, the management team of one organisation set a target to have only a particular number of incidents in the coming year (say 20). In the previous year, there were 30 major incidents, so a target of fewer for the coming year seemed appropriate. However, three quarters of the way through the year, there had already been 17 incidents. This led to people not reporting any more incidents or rating the severity of any further incidents lower than was realistic. The outcome was not what management intended, who had set the target with a view that fewer incidents should be achievable through continual improvements.

At another organisation, the target was set to find root causes in five working days because this was felt to be a good measure of effectiveness. Each team reported on how many problems were closed within five days and how many took 'too long'. I think you can guess that, with the pressure on the problem managers to report root causes within five days, this is what they did, regardless of whether cause had actually been found and confirmed, or if it was only a guess. Naturally, the expected benefits from problem management were not achieved. Too many 'solved' problems caused further incidents because the real root cause was often not established.

Metrics drive behaviour, so be clear about what behaviour you want. Metrics also drive outcomes, so be clear about where a measurement might lead. Understand what success looks like and work backwards from there to derive suitable measurements. Always ask yourself what behaviour a measurement might drive before implementing it.

Baselines for comparison

Several of the KPIs and metrics discussed here aim to highlight the progressive improvement of the process. Naturally, to see any improvement, you need to know what the starting situation is. For example, the target might be '20 per cent reduction in repeat incidents'. For this to be meaningful, you need to know how many repeat incidents you have now. Therefore, capture as much data as possible about the current measurement period before you start the implementation. This forms the baseline for measuring progress over the first phase.

The types of data most commonly captured include:

- the number of major incidents;
- the impact they have in terms of lost production time and money;
- the number of 'failed changes' being reported;
- the availability figures for each major system and how they are calculated; and
- the number of repeat incidents.

If there is a current problem management process in place, you might also be able to obtain figures on how long it takes to find root cause and what percentage of problems are actually solved.

KEY PERFORMANCE INDICATORS

Your KPIs should measure success against the objectives you have set in collaboration with your management. These 'critical success factors' are:

- finding the root cause of problems;
- putting solutions in place that eliminate problems and stop future incidents.

You will see critical success factor and key performance indicator used in different ways and sometimes confused or interchanged. If you want an understanding of the difference, a short article that might help is *The difference between critical success factors and key performance indicators* (Gilkey, 2012), which summarises the concepts as 'What must we do to be successful?' (CSFs) and 'What indicates that we're winning?' (KPIs). The Wikipedia entry for critical success factors is also quite helpful.

I think that problem management's KPIs should focus on these two key activities. I also think that you have to be efficient as well as effective at finding root cause and resolving errors. By this, I mean that real causes need to be found and then fixed completely, but also that time and resources should not be wasted to achieve these objectives. This means that there should be KPIs that tell you:

- How effective are we at finding root causes?
- How efficient are we at finding root causes?
- How effective are we at resolving errors?
- How efficient are we at resolving errors?

This approach to measuring success leads to KPIs that are not difficult to calculate and report on. I have found that management understands them quite easily and, together with a couple of additional measurements, they give a good picture of how well the process is meeting objectives.

Finding the root cause

Effective root cause analysis is measured by the percentage of root causes found for the problems investigated in a given period, or on a cumulative basis. It is calculated by taking the total number of problems and adding up those where the root cause was found and those where the root cause was not found. Problems that are either still in analysis or have not yet been started are omitted.

In my experience, well-trained problem investigation teams can find causes in about 95 per cent of cases. There will always be cases where you cannot find the cause, so the target cannot be 100 per cent.

When you are starting out, the success rate will be lower. You can deal with this either by having a lower target initially or by taking a red-amber-green (RAG) approach to KPIs during implementation. Setting lower targets is often not acceptable to management, so it might be better to use the RAG method and apply it to all the KPIs. I explain how this works at the end of this section.

Measuring the **efficiency of the process** is also not difficult. Efficiency is about finding the root cause as quickly as possible, so that problems can be resolved as quickly as possible. This reduces the risk exposure and uses valuable resources sparingly, so that problem investigations do not become a burden on the SME teams. The measurement is the time taken to find the root cause, excluding those problems for which you cannot find the root cause, those still in investigation and those not yet started. To do this, you need a timer in your toolset that captures the time when analysis starts and when the root cause has been confirmed.

Apart from the behavioural issue raised earlier, there is another issue to consider. Sometimes, uncovering the underlying cause of a problem can take quite a long time. While many problems can be investigated and their cause found within about five working days, my experience has shown that roughly 20 per cent of problems will be more complex, which is why I recommend that this KPI should be expressed with two factors. Firstly, set a target time to find cause. Second, set a threshold for what percentage of problems has to meet the target. I find that five working days is a good target time and 80 per cent is a good threshold to meet. You can set RAG statuses around these two measures during implementation as well.

The acceptable period for an investigation varies between organisations. Some will find five days far too long, others will be perfectly happy with a three-month investigation time-frame. In the former situation, you need to use the five-day argument (see below) to explain and keep stakeholders engaged with effective communication. In the latter, the effectiveness of structured methods can considerably shorten investigations and, over time, expectations will fall into line with what you are capable of delivering.

Five days is usually a good minimum to aim at for several reasons. Firstly, it can take up to 24 hours to take on a problem, gather the investigation team and run the first session. Another day usually goes by with gathering more information, performing additional analysis and reporting back from the team to the problem manager. It normally takes a further day or two to agree the root cause and perform a conclusive test to confirm the cause.

Larger problems might require vendor engagement, quite a lot of additional information to be gathered and a larger number of possible causes to be worked through and eliminated.

It is more important to be right than to be quick. You need to be right all the time, while you need to get to the cause quickly as much as possible. You can often be both, but you must not sacrifice being right for being quick.

Do not stop at maintaining your agreed ratio between normal and complex problems. Measure complex problems as a separate group and develop metrics around how they are processed. Do longer problems fall into particular categories or relate to specific applications? Is there an issue with a particular team that routinely take longer to find causes than other groups? Do you have a case to improve monitoring or data capture in certain areas, to provide better information for problem-solving? Can you drive your ratio higher over time and move the threshold up to a new level?

Know when to stop. If you reach five working days and the cause has not been found, you need to ask yourself whether it is because this is a complex problem or because there simply is not enough information to allow the cause to be found? This means you can use the target time as a decision point to agree whether a cause is likely to be found or not.

If you prioritise problems, you can keep the same time targets but allow lower priority problems to wait longer before they are investigated. You can leave all targets the same because these problems should be simpler, need smaller teams to investigate and can be assigned out to specific SME teams, provided they have training in structured methods. I have found that lower priority problems tend to wait for investigation in the early stages of an implementation because there are not enough trained staff to run effective investigations until some time has been invested in training for SME teams. Later, ways are found to run these investigations effectively and KPIs start to be enforced.

Resolving errors

Similar to finding root causes, implementing solutions can be measured fairly easily. Firstly, for every problem where the cause is known, how many have had solutions implemented? Secondly, how many of those implementations have met their agreed target implementation dates?

Calculate the first by taking the total number of problems with known causes and deducting those where either a solution was not found or a solution was not accepted for implementation. The threshold or target might be lower than you think. This is because there are situations where a solution is not accepted, perhaps because it costs too much or will take too long to apply. Other reasons for not proceeding might include that the application in question is being replaced, the business line using it is undergoing significant change, or a pending upgrade will fix the problem by removing the cause in another way.

While the total number of solutions implemented should still be reported on, the challenge is deciding what is a suitable target. I have found that the best metric to report is the percentage of problems closed and fully resolved because over time the reasons given for not implementing a solution are overcome and the problem is solved. For example, the pending upgrade is delivered and the problem can be proven to have been eliminated.

The second measurement also needs careful handling. Some solutions are a simple change to apply a patch or change a configuration. Others are major development projects. Therefore, it is not possible to set a firm target time for solutions. The best approach is to take the agreed implementation target date for each and track how many meet their targets and how many run over time.

There are many factors involved in whether solutions are implemented, so I do not find it to be a satisfactory KPI to report. Even closure of problems is difficult. Instead, I tend to focus on the second KPI, that is, how many problems are being resolved by their agreed due dates. I find this to be very good at driving effective solution implementations and opening up the opportunity for a good discussion about how long specific problems are taking to close.

Avoiding recurring problems

A recurring problem is one that has been closed as solved, but it causes further incidents. If you get one of these, either you have not found the real cause (you might have just fixed a symptom) or the fix you applied was incorrect. This is poor problem management because the process has failed to work as designed. The KPI for this is simple: it is just the number of recurring problems. The target is also simple. It should be zero.

The challenge is how to confirm that you have a recurring problem. Often, the service desk will continue to log incidents of the same type, where the symptoms present in the same way as previously seen. Some toolsets have a check box to indicate if a problem is a repeat. Naturally, any use of this checkbox should be reviewed to make sure it is used properly.

A good way to check whether a problem is recurring is to look for new incidents linked to closed problems. This is either due to an incorrect assignment or because service desk staff, perhaps using their knowledge base of incident symptoms, are accurately highlighting a causal link between further incidents and a problem thought to have been solved. If the assignment proves to be correct, the problem is not solved and you have a recurrence.

Reducing incidents

The overall objective of problem management is to improve stability by reducing the number and impact of incidents affecting services. It follows that a key (and obvious) performance indicator for problem management is to measure the reduction in incidents over a period. In my experience and in spite of the behavioural example given above, this number is often the only measure management wants to know about.

Usually, it is just the raw number of incidents, even though a reduction in overall duration of incident impact is a better indicator. A reduction in overall impact could be achieved through a combination of faster service restoration and a reduction in the number of incidents. In other words, there are fewer, shorter incidents.

As I mentioned in Section 1, you can restore service more quickly with more or better incident management, while problem management is the only way to reduce the overall number of incidents. The reduction in impact is therefore a KPI for incident and problem management working together. While it does not measure problem management specifically, it is well worth considering as a service KPI in more mature organisations.

Unfortunately, reducing incidents can be a challenging KPI to work with. You can attribute the reduction in incidents to many things, including people 'playing the system' by reporting fewer, of course. How do we know whether other factors, such as random variation, a big new system implementation or better accuracy and record keeping, affected the number of incidents in any given period? Therefore, it can be difficult to credit problem management specifically with any reduction. Careful attention to detail when tying specific incidents to accurate causes is probably the most effective approach to this common measurement.

The calculation itself is straightforward. It is simply to record the number of incidents occurring in a period and compare it with the number in the previous period.

I see regular comments about how reductions in the number of incidents can never be achieved because change continually introduces new incidents. Only in a change freeze can this objective be realised. I do not accept this argument. Change should not introduce new incidents if problem management has identified their causes and eliminated them. If it is effective, problem management should be progressively eliminating this introduced instability, until change no longer leads to incidents. See Chapter 6 for a discussion of change as a root cause.

It is possible to prove that problem management is reducing incidents once you have enough data. All you need to do is keep track of the size of the backlog of open problems and graph it against the number of new incidents raised in the same period. In Chapter 14, I describe the findings from a colleague who did this. As problems were closed and the backlog of solution implementations went down, so did the number of new incidents. In other words, as problems were eliminated, the incidents they were causing stopped.

Eliminating recurring incidents

Another common KPI for problem management is to reduce the number of recurring or repeat incidents. I take 'repeat' to mean the same incident happening again. Until a problem is solved, you should expect incidents to recur because their cause has not been eliminated. This situation implies one of three things:

- A problem is being worked on, but has not been fixed.
- It is a new situation and a problem investigation has not started.
- It is thought that the problem was fixed, but apparently it has not been.

If the latter is the case, you have a recurring problem, as discussed above. If you have one of the former, this situation is as expected. I find it difficult to justify the value of this KPI and I do not recommend it.

Improving service availability

I include service availability as a problem management KPI as well. Effective problem management is about preventing incidents, but how do you report on incidents that have not happened? A practical approach is to use availability to show that incidents are not occurring. Availability statistics essentially report on the time when systems have not been affected by incidents. The target you set depends on what your current availability measurements are and how accurate they are. If you are already at 99.99 per cent, you might not see much impact. Few organisations without effective problem management achieve that sort of target, however.

Availability metrics should already be available, so all you require is a target improvement figure for the period.

Even if you do not have this specific KPI, there is value in periodically reporting on incidents that have **not** recurred since a problem was resolved. It might be tricky to do, of course, and care is needed to exclude those incidents that have only happened once and never again, even though a fix has not been found. A list of problems closed in the period with the number of incidents related to each can be quite valuable.

Example KPIs

Table 7.1 shows my shortlist of recommended KPIs. The RAG columns are discussed below.

Table 7.1 Suggested KPIs

ID	Description	Target	RAG period 1	RAG period 2
KPI 1	Percentage of root cause being found	For major problems, 95% of root causes will be found	≥ 90% Green ≥ 85% Amber < 85% Red	≥ 95% Green ≥ 90% Amber < 90% Red
KPI 2	Percentage root cause found within 5 working days	For major problems, root cause will be found within 5 working days 80% of the time	≥ 70% Green ≥ 60% Amber < 60% Red	≥ 80% Green ≥ 70% Amber < 70% Red
KPI 3	Number of recurring problems	For major problems, zero recurring problems	$n < 3$ Green $3 \leq n < 5$ Amber $n \geq 5$ Red	$n < 1$ Green $1 \leq n < 3$ Amber $n \geq 3$ Red
KPI 4	Percentage of problems resolved within agreed time-frame	For major problems, 90% of problems will be resolved in the time-frame agreed by management	≥ 80% Green ≥ 70% Amber < 70% Red	≥ 90% Green ≥ 80% Amber < 80% Red
KPI 5	Percentage reduction in incidents from agreed baseline	For major incidents, 25% reduction in incidents per period	≥ 20% Green ≥ 15% Amber < 15% Red	≥ 25% Green ≥ 20% Amber < 20% Red
KPI 6	Percentage increase in availability	For critical systems, 3% increase in availability, from 95% to 98% (for example)	≥ 2% Green ≥ 1% Amber < 1% Red	≥ 3% Green ≥ 2% Amber < 2% Red

Measuring KPIs during implementation

Each KPI shown in Table 7.1 has its target set and is tracked through the implementation using a RAG system. The idea is that, as the implementation progresses through the agreed phases in the plan, the capability of problem management improves and the thresholds set for each colour tighten up, until the final targets are being reported against. In other words, when just starting out, the thresholds are quite loose, in recognition that it takes time to get the correct processes and methods in place and get everyone trained and on-board with the approach. The measures then tighten over time, until in one or two periods (perhaps 18 months to two years), the agreed final targets are being met.

For example, set the target at the level you want to achieve when you are fully mature and the process is working well, say at 95 per cent. Then set 85 per cent as green, 75 to 85 per cent as amber, and below 75 per cent as red. Then simply report the RAG status.

Agree the RAG for each KPI for each phase of the implementation as part of the planning process. As discussed in Chapter 4, do not allow the process to be judged against final targets when just getting started because it will look like failure. Similarly, be tough on continually raising the bar as the process matures, so that the organisation can see that continual improvement is built into the implementation. If you hit targets easily, raise the bar faster.

Governing KPIs

An effective way to formalise agreed KPIs and metrics is to incorporate them into service level agreements (SLAs) or operational level agreements (OLAs), if you have them. If not, then it is beyond the scope of your implementation to introduce the concept. Instead, put together your own reports for implementation progress and then for demonstrating your performance against KPIs, as discussed below. Your audience will be the PAB, if you have one, but more importantly, your IT management group – the people who approved your business case to proceed. They will want to see how successful you are and what impact you are having.

Look at linking your KPIs upwards to your organisation's objectives. It is professional behaviour to understand the 'cascade' of KPIs from the organisation or business level, to IT and on to the operational process or function (here, problem management). Your KPIs should align and support the organisational objectives up through the levels. You will actually find it quite simple to do this, as long as stability of service delivery and effective risk management are included at the IT level.

Tie KPIs downwards to individuals and teams as well. To meet your KPIs, each problem manager needs to meet them individually because the results aggregate. By holding accountability for behaviour and results at the team level, all can agree on what the targets are and then everyone can self-check their performance in real time. For best results, do this as a development opportunity and not as an exercise in micro-management.

For more information on governing KPIs, look at the strategy mapping work by Kaplan and Norton (2001). Their book on balanced score cards is also useful to read about KPIs and the importance of why we measure what we measure (Kaplan and Norton, 1996).

METRICS

Use **operational metrics** to manage the problem management function, its people and its activities. I covered the implementation metrics in Chapter 4, so please include them as well, especially the survey and assessment questionnaire ideas I listed. Internal customer satisfaction surveys that include customer feedback ('voice of the customer' in Six Sigma terms) are very useful, and so are staff surveys, because they provide some concrete facts about what people understand about the process, the level of maturity, how far along they think they are, and so on.

Operational metrics focus on monitoring the process, looking for bottlenecks, areas of concern, the workload balance between problem managers or areas and anything unusual that needs follow-up or escalation. They also allow the measurement of different target areas in a staged implementation, contrasting different parts of an organisation and helping to focus improvement efforts where needed. These metrics rely on time stamps and status codes included in your toolset (Section 3 has a summary of these for each step in the process). The most important metrics to gather are about the progress of problems through the process.

Investigation metrics start with the handover from incident management, which should be timely and effective. However, problems should also be picked up in a timely manner. As well as measuring how long problems take to be accepted, once raised, it is useful to know how long it takes between assigning a problem to a problem manager and the start of actual investigation work. Therefore, it is important to track and report daily on problems sitting in draft or assigned, which equates to no progress. This second part of the measurement can be difficult if you do not have a specific 'assigned' state, which the problem manager moves the problem to before investigation begins.

You should be able to measure how long root cause investigations take, individually and on average. You need this to know how you are tracking against your KPIs, but also to ensure that individuals are being effective. The average time to root cause for each problem manager can highlight development opportunities, as well as finding individuals who are either very good or who might be cutting corners or 'cherry-picking' easy problems and avoiding tough ones. Exception reporting on excessive time for problems sitting in root cause analysis is also useful.

Linked to the previous metric is the raw number of problems where the root cause has been found versus those where it has not. This is for the KPI, but is also useful to identify areas for improvement in the overall process.

Resolution metrics should include the time taken from when the root cause is found to when a solution is approved, and how long the solution implementation takes. In addition to the KPI measurement against agreed implementation times, absolute durations are also useful, particularly to contrast between resolver teams, applications or technology areas. Do not forget to measure vendors as well because this is a key element of their management. Again, exception reporting on long-running implementations is useful, as is reporting and follow-up on unexplained implementation date shifts.

Volume-based metrics include the number of problems per problem manager, sorted by priority and where they are in the process. It is useful to have a breakdown of problems by stage (root cause analysis, resolution implementation, pending, and so on) because this shows up bottlenecks in the process, as well as potential inefficiencies in the team. Too many problems in resolution point to a weakness in getting problems solved and closed. A high proportion of problems in root cause analysis probably indicates a resource issue more than ineffective analysis because many of these will probably be waiting for investigation to start. Some might have started and stalled, others might be lengthy investigations, while the majority are progressing normally, but there are more problems than the team can reasonably handle.

The overall volume of problems in progress is a mandatory metric as well. It is best to capture it monthly, so that trends can be tracked. Stacked bars showing the split by priority can also show whether problems of a particular priority (usually low priority) are piling up. I have seen this in every implementation I have been involved in or observed and I discuss how to address it in Chapter 4.

A key aspect of tracking metrics is that it needs to happen frequently. Depending on the particular metric, a daily status report or health check is a much better option than a weekly or monthly report. Early awareness is often vital to catch exceptions or developing issues. Depending on your toolset, it might be possible to send alerts to individual problem managers when thresholds are exceeded, including a link to the problem record in question.

For every metric that is chosen, decide at the same time the threshold for alerting, the frequency of reporting, the audience, the method of delivery and how historical data will be kept to produce trend analysis over time, or between groups or geographies.

Operational metrics are mainly for internal use. They are useful to share with your team and with your direct management, but senior management and your customers might not find them interesting, so do not include them in external reporting.

The **analytical metrics** that come out of problem investigations are definitely of interest to customers and management. The information they reveal feeds into proactive problem management and CSI. The major ones are:

- Types and numbers of root causes found, either across the organisation, per individual area or per support group.

- Root cause types by application or technology, especially if shown with the number and severity of incidents for that item in the same period.

- Average time to implement solutions, also useful when broken down by area or resolver group. Highlight outliers for special attention.

- Potentially, if there is interest, failed changes grouped by their actual root causes and similar data captured for projects, releases and other implementations that have caused problems.

Together with KPIs, these analytical metrics form the primary content of your reporting to senior management and customers.

REPORTING

Reporting is where measurement and communication intersect. Any reporting you publish needs to consider the standard questions for all communication:

- Who is the audience?
- What do they already know?
- What is the message I am seeking to get across?
- Do I know what they want to know? Have I asked them?

My point is that a report is communication and if you do not understand your audience, the report will not communicate effectively. You need to tell a meaningful story.

> It does not matter if your reports are stand-alone or included in more general operational reporting – you always need to keep control of the content and make sure you are saying something useful. If your data is included with incident and change data, which is being reported in fairly meaningless tables or charts, do not fall into line. Make your reporting meaningful.

For problem management, most audiences want to know whether problem management is working for them, that their risks are being addressed and that problem causes are being found and fixed. Your reporting should address these questions and then go on to tell them additional things, such as whether fixes are being delayed due to lack of engagement of the resolver groups, and what types of problems are occurring in their operating environment.

Meaningful reporting on the effectiveness of problem management is much more useful than showing lists of problems and graphs of numbers. There is nothing worse than presenting numbers that do not mean anything to their intended audience. Allow me to illustrate.

Figure 7.1 is an example of a type of graph that I have often seen used to present to senior management. It is hard to see what the message might be.

Figure 7.1 Problems opened per month

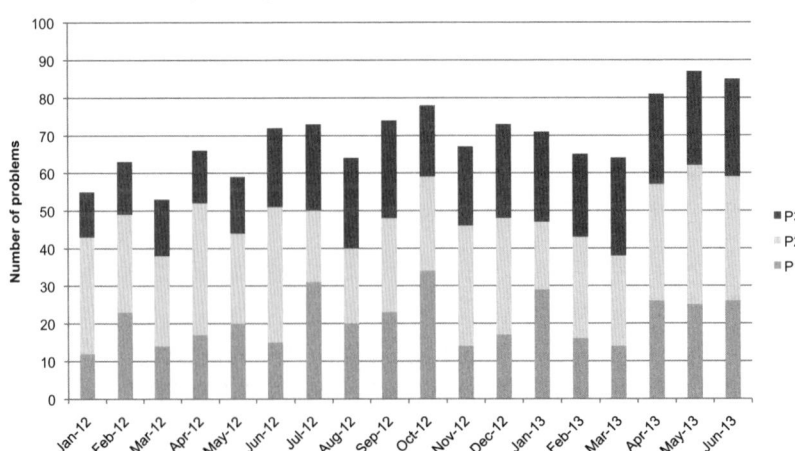

However, the chart in Figure 7.2 has a message. It says what is going wrong and where, and management can readily understand that there is an issue with the process documentation for the Vendor Order System, for example.

You need to decide at what level you want to report on deferred problems (root cause not found, not resolved, resources or funding pending, disinvest) in order to maintain their visibility. It is useful to keep senior management aware of pending problems because it is good risk management practice as previously discussed.

As well as statistical and informational reporting, stakeholders usually want to see summaries of individual major problem investigations. The focus should be on problems that have investigated high-profile incidents, as well as good proactive investigations that have removed risks from the environment. Figure 7.3 is an example status report.

The fields you include are the same as I set out in the communications section of Chapter 6. For completeness, I also include a customer or business impact assessment (CIA or BIA) as part of every problem report, even though it is usually a feature of incident reporting.

Figure 7.2 Current top-five root causes by application

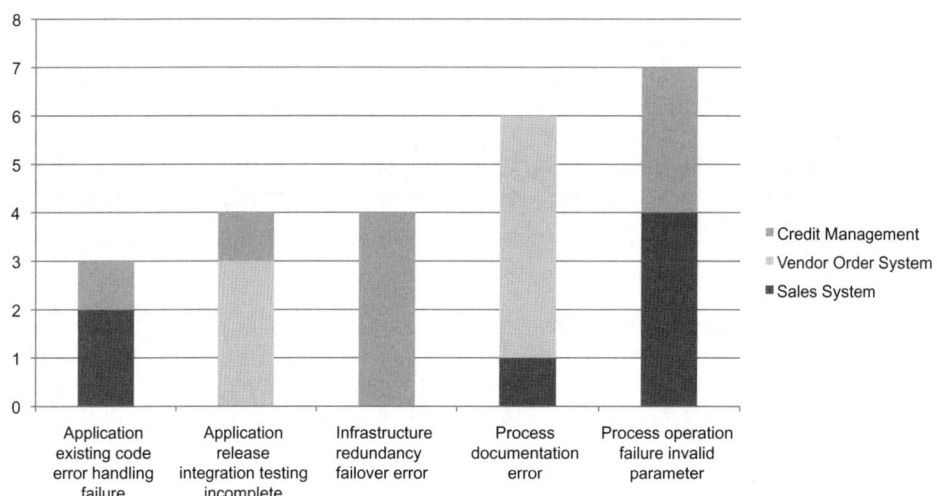

Figure 7.3 Sample problem status report

Date		Problem no.		Priority		Status	
Problem statement							
Business impact							
Root cause description							
Root cause codes							
Latest update							

Action	Due date	Owner

Wherever possible, avoid manual reports. Depending on your tools, extract all the information from key fields in the toolset via a report writer, a macro or through the native capability of the tool itself. While this eliminates the effort that goes into manual reporting, it requires that the information put into the toolset is good enough for your audience. In your training and operating instructions for staff, it is necessary to give clear instructions about what information goes where, and to what standard of quality.

Adopt standardised formatting. A consistent look and feel makes information easier to access and digest for the audience. Consider also making your standard reports available through your self-service portal, so that service managers and business relationship managers can pull out problem reports whenever they need to talk to their customers.

8   TOOL REQUIREMENTS

The tools that you use to support the problem management process will very likely be chosen as part of the selection of an overall service management suite of tools. This short chapter aims to give you some guidance about what to look for and what modifications might need to be made in a new or existing tool to better support problem management. Specific support is generally not included in these service management suites for structured root cause analysis, to develop and record processes and workflows and to analyse data. More specialised tools that can be used for these types of applications are covered in Section 3 as these topics come up.

It is possible to do problem management without a formal toolset – it is just harder and more time-consuming. Although a manual approach might be viable in a small organisation, a good toolset is essential if your organisation is larger.

There are many good tools out there, but rather than try to do an assessment of what is available in the market that will quickly date, it is probably more helpful to focus instead on the key features and requirements needed to support problem management effectively.

The tool should be configurable to support your process. If you have to make significant process changes to fit how the tool works, it is probably not suitable for supporting problem management.

Tools should be easy to adapt without introducing poor performance due to all the overhead processing you have introduced, or difficulty in applying new vendor releases. I have seen this happen twice on different, industry-leading platforms, so try to keep modifications to a minimum, look for a tool that you can change mainly through straightforward configuration updates and work with your vendor to ensure that what you are doing is not going to get you into future difficulties.

If you find that you cannot fit your process into how a specific tool works and it is one of the mainstream ones, you might want to consider if your process is the issue. Work through Section 3 and check that you are not too far away from what I consider to be a standard approach to problem management before going any further with your tool selection.

Any tool you choose should be easy to use and be responsive. It should be easy and quick to raise a problem and enter data, as well as to see at what stage the problem is, who is accountable and who is working on what.

Many tools are integrated service management suites that include problem management. This introduces a risk because the tool becomes critical and a potential single point of failure. Look out for performance issues if one tool does everything. You might want to consider including reliability, resilience and performance in your assessment criteria.

The toolset needs to support problem management from two perspectives: managing the workflow and managing the information.

MANAGING THE WORKFLOW

There should be clear states or statuses throughout the workflow, so you know at what stage in the process each problem investigation is.

I suggest the following states (it does not matter what they are called, as long as it is clear to you which part of the process that the state represents):

- New – the problem has been raise but no one is working on it yet.
- Assigned – the problem has a problem manager (and perhaps nothing else has happened yet).
- Investigate root cause – root cause analysis is in progress.
- Find solution – you have found a root cause and now you are working on finding a solution to fix it.
- Implement solution – the fix is being implemented. You will see tools that combine this and the previous state into 'resolution' or 'known error', which makes it hard to know if you have a fix and you are implementing it, or you are still working out what can be done to fix the problem.
- Resolved – the team believes that a fix has been successfully applied and it just needs to be checked or tested in some way.
- Deferred or pending – for some reason the problem is not progressing, but should not be closed. See Chapter 15 for a full explanation of this very important state.
- Closed – the root cause has been found and a solution has been implemented. The problem should never cause an incident again. Conversely, it might be closed because it is cancelled for some reason, such as it is a duplicate of another or has been raised in error and is not a problem that needs to be investigated.

Many tools will not support this list 'out of the box'; however, a good tool should be configurable to add states or, if not, you should be able to adapt those it has to represent most of them. You might need to think carefully before adopting a tool that is not configurable and does not have at least most of these states.

A good tool should support the problem logging process effectively. When raising a reactive problem, it should auto-populate the new problem record with key data from the incident record, as well as link the two together. This is common sense and most tools these days should support this function. Having said that, tools should not automatically generate problem records when incidents are resolved, for the reasons covered in Chapter 11. Only accept such a tool if this feature can be disabled.

As well as linking problem records to an incident as noted above, it should be possible to link problems to other incidents, to other problems and to knowledge base content. In fact, the more linkage types the tool supports, the better (see Chapter 6). In reality, most problems investigate the cause of multiple incidents and it is best if they can all be linked correctly. This implies that some sort of list functionality is a requirement. Similarly, you might need to link one problem to another. This can happen when one problem investigation is in progress and another similar problem is found that might benefit from the same solution. It is not all that uncommon in reality, but is admittedly more of a 'nice to have' than a requirement. However, as you become more advanced, you will start to come across situations where you find proactive problems that emerge during the investigation or resolution of reactive problems. In this case, it is very handy to be able to raise and link a new problem record from an existing one.

Many tools allow a problem to be linked to only one change. This might be an interpretation of the ITIL® recommended workflow, which seems to imply that the best process is to raise a change to implement the fix. I think some toolmakers have forgotten that ITIL® is guidance and high level at that. In the real world, problems often require the implementation of multiple changes to address all the issues that come out of problem investigations. This means that your toolset should ideally have the capability to link to multiple changes. In addition, as problem investigations often result from changes that have led to incidents, it is handy to be able to link to these changes as well, to make access to information simpler.

It should be possible to allocate sub-units of work while maintaining ownership of the overall problem record. You should not be forced to pass the problem ownership around to get work done – problems quickly get lost and the continuity of ownership is broken. Tools should therefore have the ability to assign and track tasks related to a problem. I have often observed a tendency for SMEs to close the tasks they have assigned to them, even if the work is incomplete. To counter this, there should be a capability to have a review step in tasks, so that they can be referred back to the problem manager before closure.

To improve governance, a history of how the problem record has been changed is very useful, including who moved it on from one state to another and when the problem or sub-tasks have been reassigned. This is especially useful to keep control of another commonly seen behaviour, that of 'pass the parcel' from one group or one person to another. A reassignment counter is needed for this. You also need the ability to correlate tasks across different problems, to extract all the tasks assigned to one individual, support group, development team or vendor, to allow good workload management and good conversations about progress and results.

It is also very useful to have the ability to set target, reminder and follow-up dates for tasks and for problems in particular states. For example, the ability to enter a review date for problems in the pending state, as well as for problems awaiting the implementation of a solution by a third party supports the process very effectively.

MANAGING THE INFORMATION

Any tool should provide a place to record:

- the root cause;
- contributing factors;
- workarounds found either during the incident or the problem investigation;
- the resolution that is or will be implemented;
- closure information;
- the problem manager owning the problem;
- all the SMEs working on it.

In addition, there should be a log or journal area to make notes, provide updates and capture information that comes out of analysis sessions and the investigation process.

Performance measurement data must also be captured, in particular time stamps. It is essential to know how long process steps take, particularly how long it takes to find the root cause and how long problems wait before they are picked up for investigation. The tool must support the process measurements and KPIs related to measuring that are set out in Chapter 7.

Problem management tools should be as much about getting the data out as getting it recorded in the first place. Fortunately, most modern tools take an information- or knowledge-based view. In other words, as well as facilitating the flow of the process, they avoid trapping useful information in formats that are difficult to extract. For example, instead of maintaining all the information in individual problem records accessed via the problem number, the data displayed on forms is actually stored in a fully searchable database.

In Chapter 6, I talked about my view of how incident, problem and knowledge management should ideally interact. I have not seen a tool that supports this integration 'out of the box'. Perhaps this will change as the importance of this integration is recognised. As well as the capability for sharing information between incidents, problems and knowledge articles, the ability to extract and correlate data for proactive problem management and CSI is absolutely essential. It is also essential that data sharing is possible between the problem system and the service desk and between configuration, change and availability management systems.

One other essential tool requirement that follows from this integrated approach to data is an ability to create known error records without a problem record. There are two use cases for this, both mentioned in Chapter 6. One is the relationship between release management and known errors, while the other is how workarounds develop mainly during incident resolution, not during problem investigation.

The benefits of good problem management will not be achievable if the tool does not support good classification. Classifications need to be configurable and organised into a hierarchy of codes and sub-codes. Three or four levels are ideal.

REPORTING AND COMMUNICATION

The tool should make data easily available for reporting and communication. In particular, it should be possible to set up report templates that extract key information to generate formal and informal problem status reports, as detailed in Chapter 6. Targeting these reports through easy-to-set-up address lists should be possible, as well as some sort of self-service for stakeholders, perhaps by offering a way for stakeholders to subscribe to the specific information feeds they want to hear about.

Exposing information in dashboards and simple extraction of data for performance measurement against KPIs and other metrics (see Chapter 7) should also all be easy to set up and automate. An option to extract data for external manipulation in sophisticated analysis and reporting tools is an advantage.

Running reports should not have an impact on a tool's performance for logging and tracking problems and any other processes it supports, such as incident and change management. This might need to be checked as part of the selection process.

AIDS TO SELECTION

PinkVERIFY™ is one of a number of services that assess toolsets for adherence to ITIL®'s problem management best practice. It is a starting point for reviewing any tool that you are assessing for suitability. While I do not necessarily accept that ITIL® has the ideal model for problem management, it is a good approach to setting a baseline for assessment. The assessment criteria form is particularly useful.

If you wish to go into the tool selection topic in greater depth, Robert Falkowitz's book, *IT Tools For The Business When The Business Is IT*, is both comprehensive and easy to read (Falkowitz, 2011).

Most tool vendors will have a user forum, or there might be an 'unofficial' one, which should provide enough information to gauge how well the tool in question is viewed by those already using it, as well as address any shortcomings or hot topics. As you get closer to picking a toolset, consider joining one or more of these. Once you select a tool, it makes sense to remain engaged in the user forum so that you can contribute to and guide the direction of the tool's development.

9 WHERE NEXT FOR PROBLEM MANAGEMENT?

I want to close Section 2 by considering how to extend and further improve the process in a mature problem management organisation. As problem management matures in the IT organisation, success should mean that the volume of reactive problems starts to decrease. This will initially free up time to devote to proactive problem investigations, but eventually even these problems will reduce. At that point, there is a need to think about long-term goals and develop a method of working for the future, where a smaller team is supporting a more stable production environment with fewer problems. The central team, of course, would still manage large, cross-functional problems, but there will be opportunities to extend problem management into other areas such a business operations.

PROBLEM MANAGEMENT WITHIN IT

The problem management team will focus more on coaching and governance of the process as opposed to doing problem management because there will be more people embedded in the service support and development teams with the necessary skills and attitudes to run their own investigations, without calling on the problem management team itself. You will need fewer problem managers and those you have can focus on additional ways to add value.

Continual service improvement

I spoke about continual service improvement (CSI) earlier and this is one area to which problem analysis skills can be applied. CSI cuts across many areas of IT and organisations do not always have a dedicated function for it. Incorporating CSI responsibilities into the problem management team is straightforward due to the natural fit of skills and attitudes. CSI can start to generate real value straight away.

Software development, agile and DevOps

A second way to apply problem management skills is to get problem management happening early in the development life cycle. Barry Corless, from Global Knowledge, made this point at an ITSMF problem management day in 2012. Starting with feeding lessons learned from current problem investigations back into the development cycle, it is possible to address future problems as early as the design stage. As new applications are prepared for going live, start applying incident and problem management in user acceptance testing. Then, as the application goes into production, errors will already have workarounds available, or will already be fixed, and the known error database will already be available and usable by support teams.

Problem management applies in agile development environments as well. It has been said that agility needs stability or, put another way, you cannot be agile when you are fragile. What this means is that agile development works best in an environment from which major problems have been eliminated. This is the key deliverable of problem management. One approach that I have seen work is the concept of a 'licence to develop'. Agile development can continue as long as service interruptions due to introduced bugs are limited. If the business raises concerns that the stability of the application is impacting their ability to service customers, the 'licence' can be suspended and support teams need to stop new deployments, analyse the cause of the instability and correct it. Once stability has been confirmed, they get their licence back and can return to their rapid deployment approach.

To the best of my knowledge, DevOps does not include a built-in problem-solving methodology, any more than other approaches to supporting production environments. The basic idea of DevOps is that application development, infrastructure and application support teams are essentially one team, with responsibility for developing, deploying and supporting applications and the environment they run on. The tools marketed to support DevOps seem to be generally rapid deployment tools, focused on automating the release management cycle. There is no reason to expect that the adoption of this approach to service support leaves no requirement for problem management. It certainly does; it just means that all team members need problem management skills and attitudes built in.

First fault problem-solving

In agile environments, perhaps supported using DevOps methods, it pays to get things right the first time wherever possible. This is where an alternative problem management approach known as First Fault Problem-solving can be very effective. Proposed by Dan Skwire, a colleague based in Florida, USA, the general idea is that applications and infrastructure are fully instrumented, so that any failure is reported along with enough information to show immediately what went wrong and how to fix it. This is not unlike how many early IT systems were constructed. Taken to the next level, systems become fully fault tolerant and self-correcting. It is an interesting idea and well worth looking into. I have included his book in the references.

Value streams and Lean applied to IT

Proactive problem management and Lean have a lot in common. Both approaches are looking at improving systems, services and operations by eliminating problems or 'waste'. For me, one of the most interesting lessons from Lean and Lean Six Sigma is the idea of value streams. This idea helped me to think about services in a more comprehensive way and showed how problem management could extend across the whole landscape of suppliers, vendors, service organisations, the internal organisation, consultants and customers. Everyone contributes to the value of the service and there are possibilities for problems to occur at any point in the value stream, or at multiple points at the same time. Problem management can help upstream and downstream processes, starting with your internal organisation, to improve the overall value realisation for your business customers. In the classic book *Lean Thinking*, Womack and Jones make a point about taking care when defining value. You need to ask the customer what they value; there is no way forward from making assumptions (Womack and Jones, 2003, p.31).

So, a next step for your problem management organisation could be to start to engage with your 'upstream' suppliers and vendors to help them solve problems that are impacting you.

This approach differs from common problem process thinking, where it is assumed that problems that are outside your control are not in scope for problem-solving. For example, if you have an incident caused by a faulty server component, how the server vendor makes its components is not something that would be rewarding to investigate. While this assumption is generally true and helps people focus on when to solve problems and when to mitigate them, it should not be a strict constraint. You might not be able to justify the time and cost of using your resources to help that server vendor improve their manufacturing, but you might be able to identify cases where it is worthwhile talking to a supplier about your concerns. A good example might be working with the managed service data centre provider used to host your internet presence to improve the management capabilities for their hosts.

CASE STUDY

When thinking about this front-to-back approach, do not forget to reach forward towards your customers as well as back towards your suppliers. An example from my direct experience happened during a problem investigation into a batch process that was missing its 4 a.m. SLA target. While looking at what was causing the processing to take longer, we also asked the customer why the SLA was set to 4 a.m. It turned out that it was a legacy that was set when the customer did not trust IT to deliver their output when they needed it at 8 a.m., due to a history of failures. These failures had been addressed some time ago, but the SLA was not updated. The longer processing that was now happening was actually due to increased business volumes and not failures. Moving the SLA target to 6 a.m. solved the problem. Breaching an SLA is not a problem at all if the SLA is wrong or out of date. It pays to check, so look forward in the value stream and talk to your customers as well.

Lean can also be applied to the problem management process itself. The review task that forms part of phase two of your implementation plan is a good place to do this. One of the things that Lean identifies as waste that should be eliminated is rework. This is where things are not made properly or done correctly and must be sent back to be fixed. In the problem process, as expected, this is where the root cause is not found or solutions are not acceptable and the problem is sent back for rework (see Chapter 15 for more on this). Lean's concept of inventory (which should be minimised) equates to the backlog of problems either waiting for investigation or waiting for resolution. An example of how effective Lean can be in improving your processes is included in Chapter 14.

PROBLEM MANAGEMENT OUTSIDE IT

Before I started researching this book, I was not aware of how entrenched problem management was in some organisations, particularly in the manufacturing, utilities and resource sectors. It was a reminder that the ITIL® framework adopted the existing practice of problem management. It became obvious that Kepner–Tregoe techniques were being widely applied and that the quality movement promoted problem management techniques as well. If your organisation is one of those that have adopted these methods in its business operations, you might already find useful skills and resources that you can draw on in developing problem management within IT. The quality movement is a rich source of ideas on the subject, under what they call, somewhat confusingly, 'root cause analysis', but what refers to the entire end-to-end process of finding the root cause and developing and applying solutions. They have some very good books on root cause analysis available and I have listed some of them in the references and Further reading section.

If your organisation has not already taken up these ideas, the next step for you might be to look at extending the reach of problem management outside IT and even outside the organisation. The business has problems to solve just as IT does and you can apply your problem management skills directly to solving them. The hardest part is the first step, of course, but you should be able to use your existing record of success at solving IT problems to break the ice and cross the divide. It is certainly something to think about when your team reaches the end-state level of maturity and has fewer problems to solve with IT systems and services.

Problem management should be a key component of the enterprise service management (ESM) approach, which aims to apply service management principles to general business operations. ESM mostly focuses on using workflow concepts to support defined services in business operations. There are many examples of the application of ESM, for example in the use of the release management process for new product development and deployment. What I think is lacking, however, is taking the problem management approach and applying that as well. As I said, problem management techniques are directly applicable and you should be getting involved in any ESM efforts starting in your organisation.

Another relationship to Lean

As well as applying Lean to improving problem management, the reverse also works. The proactive problem management process can directly integrate with your business's improvement programmes. Process improvement methods like Lean might benefit from the inclusion of problem management to find and fix those problems that will not be eliminated by improving an existing process, because the process itself might be the problem. James Weiss from Kepner–Tregoe points this out in a 2012 white paper (sadly no longer available on the KT website). Problem management (specifically KT in the white paper) and process improvement practices can run side by side. Lean is for the removal of what he calls common causes, while KT is for the removal of specific causes. In other words, they are different tools for different applications.

WHERE TO NEXT FOR PROBLEM MANAGERS?

Problem managers probably will not stay in the role indefinitely. A natural consequence of needing fewer problem managers is that people will move on to other challenges. They might move to other organisations to take more senior roles, they might become consultants or they might get promoted within their organisation. In my view, problem management is a seed ground for future leaders.

The broad context of problem management involvement means that the problem manager role is a path to general management. The analytical and solution implementation skills, the collaboration and network building involved and the positive contributions to stability and effectiveness of technology systems all contribute to building a well-rounded profile for problem managers. These skills are all directly applicable to management roles.

The other path for problem managers is out of IT and into the business. In the above, I have advocated the application of problem management disciplines to solve business and operational issues. Instead of 'lending' problem managers to business lines from the central team, it is a natural step for staff to move into problem management roles directly in quality or operational teams. Putting these two suggestions together, the same skills that equip problem managers as future IT managers also makes them well placed for general management roles in any part of the business. So, the career path for problem managers is very broad, with a wide range of opportunities available to them.

SECTION 3 – PROBLEM MANAGEMENT PROCESS AND TECHNIQUES

This is a reference section that presents what I consider to be a good quality, Lean process implementation for managing problems throughout their life cycle. I start with a process overview and then summarise each process step in turn.

10 PROCESS OVERVIEW

This chapter introduces the process that I have implemented several times. It talks about the states and sub-states needed, which I think strike a good balance between being able to manage and track the process and being easy to use.

This process flow is a practical interpretation of the high-level view depicted and discussed in *ITIL Service Operation* (Cabinet Office, 2011, p.102). It is an interpretation because I think what ITIL® presents is not actually very practical. As far as possible I have mentioned where I disagree with the ITIL® process in the relevant chapters that follow. For example, I do not think I have ever run a formal major problem review. Other people might find them useful, but I cannot see how they offer any significant benefit as a routine process step.

Generally, process flows can be developed quite easily in standard flow charting tools. If you have to develop a lot of process maps and associated documentation, there are also dedicated process design tools on the market.

Each subsequent chapter will refer to this process and include a table of the entry and exit states for the problem record, what metrics should be captured, what communication should be sent, the interfaces to other process as they occur and who is involved in each step. The tables are in the format shown in Table 10.1.

Table 10.1 Key to process states and metrics

Incoming state	The state in which the problem enters this process step
Incoming sub-states	The possible sub-states
Who is involved	The people engaged in this step
Outgoing state	The state in which the problem leaves this process step
Outgoing sub-states	The possible sub-states
Time stamps	Date and time data captured for metrics
Relevant metrics	How this process step is measured
Calculations	What calculations are required to produce meaningful metrics for this process step

---

STATES

Down the right-hand side of the process diagram (Figure 10.1) is an example of the states that could be implemented in a tool to show the progress of the problem through its life cycle (Table 10.2). The only one that might need a little explanation is the deferred state, which is covered in Chapter 15. As noted in Chapter 7, keeping track of the state of problems simplifies managing and reporting on the health of the process and the problem management function itself.

Table 10.2 Process states

State	Description
Draft	A problem has been raised and is awaiting assignment to a problem manager. Duplicates and other problem records raised in error are rejected and sent for closure.
Assigned	A problem manager now owns the problem but no work has commenced.
Investigation (root cause analysis)	The root cause of the problem is being investigated. Regular status reports are sent out until the cause is found.
Error resolution	A root cause has been found and steps to resolve the problem have been agreed and are being implemented. Regular status reports are sent out until the resolution is complete.
Ready for review	The problem is at a decision point. Three exits are possible – closure, deferral and rework. If the problem is resolved, stakeholders must agree it is fixed before closure. If a cause was not found, or the resolution is not progressing for some reason, agreement is required before deferring the problem. If the decision with the stakeholders is that more actions are required (more investigation, for instance), the problem is sent back for further work.
Deferred	When a root cause cannot be found or a resolution cannot progress (no suitable fix, too expensive, waiting for retirement of the system, waiting for budget or resources etc.), the risk to business operations has not been eliminated. By agreeing to defer a problem, the stakeholders accept the risk. The deferred problem is tracked with regular updates, until the situation changes in some way so that the risk can be addressed.
Closed	The problem has been completely resolved so that it cannot cause an incident in future. Duplicates and rejected problem records are also closed.

Figure 10.1 Problem management process flow

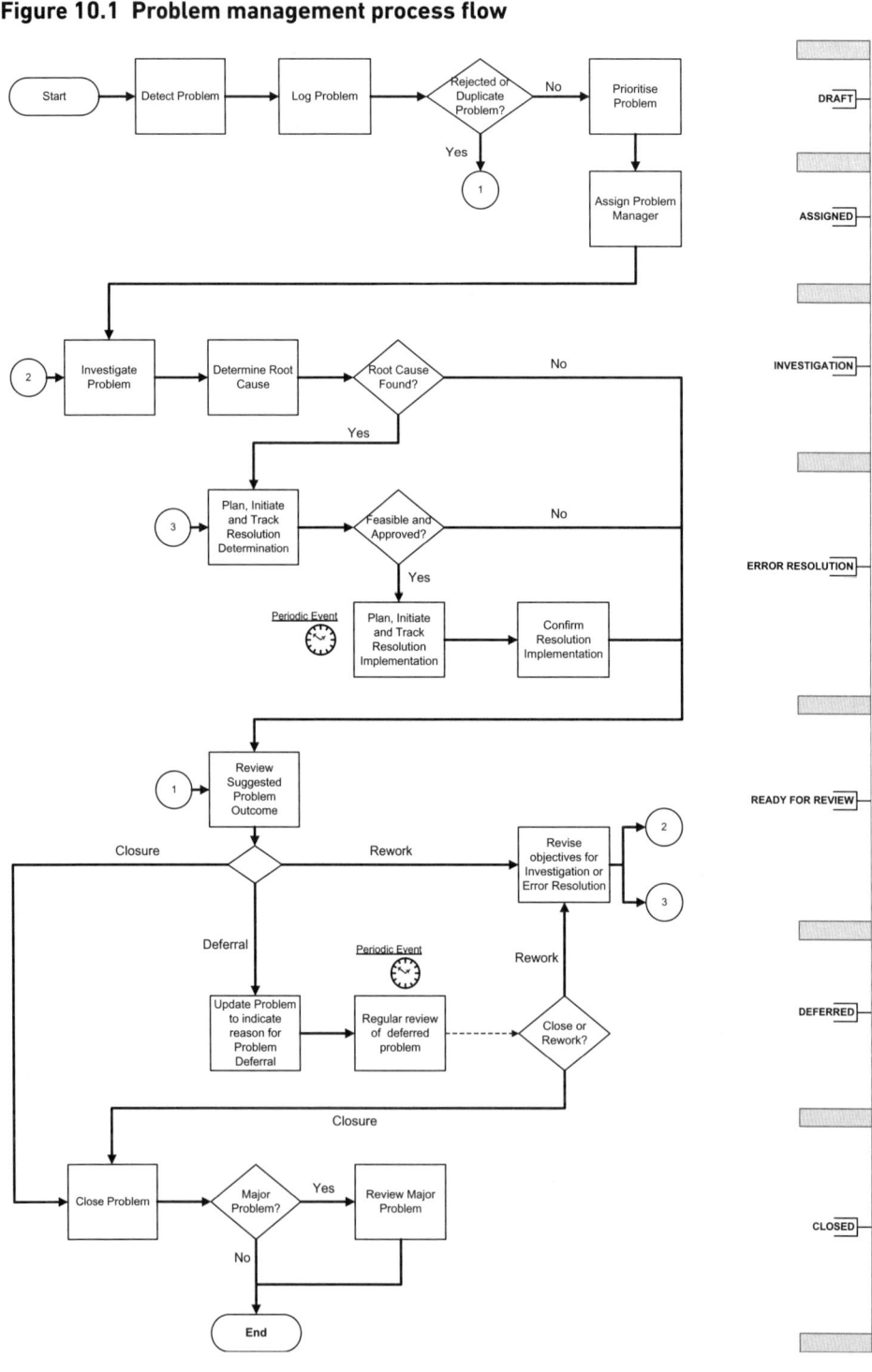

Sub-states can provide more information in certain states such as error resolution, where it might be an advantage to know whether a solution is being sought or whether it is being implemented. You do not need many sub-states, just enough to make it clear why a problem is in the state it is in. Be careful not to go too granular because this makes it difficult for busy problem managers to keep on top of updating the status of their problems. Data can only be as good as how accurately it can be kept up to date.

The key sub-states are for ready for review, deferred and closed:

- Ready for review:
    - Rejected;
    - Duplicate;
    - Root cause not found;
    - Solution not found;
    - Solution not approved;
    - Solution implemented.
- Deferred:
    - Root cause not found;
    - Solution not found;
    - Solution not approved;
    - Future upgrade pending;
    - To be retired;
    - Pending business merger, acquisition or divestment.
- Closed:
    - Resolved;
    - Rejected;
    - Duplicate.

It is essential to have time stamps in your toolset to record when problems move between states and sub-states, so that you can measure performance and highlight any process or functional issues.

11 DETECT AND LOG PROBLEMS

Table 11.1 Detect and log states and metrics

Incoming state	None
Incoming sub-states	None
Who is involved	Anyone
Outgoing state	New
Outgoing sub-states	None
Time stamps	Problem created date
Relevant metrics	None
Calculations	None

This chapter is about the process of raising problems investigation. It talks in detail about the major detection processes: raising problems reactively following an incident and finding problems proactively in the environment.

DETECTING PROBLEMS

The *ITIL Service Operation* book (Cabinet Office, 2011, pp.102–103) talks about 'detecting' problems and lists the sources as service desk, event management, incident management, proactive problem management and supplier or contractor. In reality, it is fairly simple to group how problems are found into two methods: in reaction to an incident (reactive) and all other ways of detecting problems (proactive). Let me explain.

It should be apparent that problems proposed by the service desk flow from one of the following:

- individual incidents that need further investigation;
- observation of patterns of requests or incidents that seem to point to an underlying problem;

- the service desk's management of the knowledge base that they use to address incidents and requests.

In other words, problems suggested by the service desk will be either reactive or proactive.

Similarly, incident management will either request a problem investigation into the cause of an incident that they have managed, or suggest that there is an underlying problem that might be causing a series of related incidents.

Lastly, problems detected by event management, suppliers or contractors are also either warning of a potential incident or related to an incident that has occurred.

Event management as a source for generating problems needs careful consideration. I have seen this taken to mean that an event can automatically log a problem record. It is hard to see how this can work effectively. There is a danger that multiple problem records will be auto-created. Each would need to be reviewed and a decision made about whether to progress an investigation and with what priority. It is not hard to see this process clogging up the system and overloading the problem management team, while adding no value whatsoever. ITIL® does not actually recommend this approach and I think it should be avoided.

Who can raise a problem? I suggest that anyone can request a problem investigation. A service request template could be set up for problem investigation requests. The PAB could be responsible for reviewing, accepting or rejecting and prioritising accepted problems. The requester needs to make a good case for their request and supply enough detail to allow an informed decision.

REACTIVE PROBLEM MANAGEMENT

Problems often flow from incidents that have already happened, so managing the handover from incident management is a key contributor to the effectiveness of problem management. This transition is surprisingly difficult to get working properly, even with the best intentions of all involved. Along with implementing solutions, discussed in Chapter 14, it is one of the most common bottlenecks in the process.

It is essential that incidents are handed over to problem management and the investigation starts as soon as possible. As well as addressing the credibility gap discussed under effective communications in Chapter 6, the evidence will be fresher and you usually get a better outcome. A rapid handover from incident management to problem management requires agreement between the two teams that is also supported by management. This working agreement should be clearly set out in writing, in a formal document such as an operating level agreement.

The first thing to decide is how and when the incident-to-problem handover takes place. This can be via a meeting, from a dashboard or even automatically assigned, if that suits your organisation. Preferably, incident management and problem management should jointly review incidents. Service management and operations managers should be involved as well. If you have a daily incident review call, this is an excellent forum for managing handover. A daily call works well when the volumes are manageable and it is often the best way to do it, because a lot of information can be shared at the same time. It is also excellent for building collaboration between teams.

When agreeing what incidents need problem investigations, also clearly note any incidents that are not going to be picked up and why (for example, the cause might have been found during service restoration and there is no further work to do). It is good practice to ensure that stakeholders understand when and why a problem investigation is not needed.

The incident team should make as much information as possible available to the problem manager. It is best to copy all this information automatically from the incident record when raising a problem record. As an example, this is a typical list of information required:

- The symptoms reported.
- The services affected.
- To what extent – all staff and locations, some, or specific geographies or teams?
- Any workaround implemented to restore service.
- Was the incident related to a new process or activity or a failure of current normal operations?
- Incident start and resolution times.
- The timeline of events during the incident.
- The business units impacted.
- Description of the impact.
- The triggering or technical cause.
- The resolution that restored service.
- The teams or individuals involved in restoring service.
- What systems and services were involved in the solution.
- If a root cause was found or suspected, what are the details?
- Any outstanding actions for problem follow-up.

Sometimes, information received might be garbled or summarised, leaving the problem manager with not much to go on. In this case, any missing information should be obtained as part of the first root cause analysis session. I do not recommend rejecting problems due to lack of information. This might seem good from a process point of view, but it is not a practice that makes management and customers happy.

The health of the handover process can be tracked using time stamps, such as when service is restored during the incident and when the problem investigation commences. I discussed the relevant metrics to govern incident handover in Chapter 7.

Depending on your toolset, it might be possible to send alerts to problem management when incidents are raised or resolved and ready for handover. This can help to ensure that problems are not missed.

There is tension between the needs of incident management and problem management, which must be managed effectively. For example, when service restoration demands rebooting the server, for example, while further analysis requires that the core dump should be captured first, the teams need a pre-agreed process in place for how to deal with a situation such as this. Reactive, 'fix at all costs' incident management can in fact be very costly because destroying evidence that could be essential for problem management stores up problems for the future.

Restore service quickly without introducing new risks or making the situation worse, but retain evidence for root cause analysis. However, resist holding up service restoration to do cause analysis. Document the agreed information requirements and approach to capturing data in the agreement between the teams.

Also remember that, in terms of incidents, problem management is an 'after the event' activity. Do not try to do problem analysis during an incident. Focus on restoring service. Everyone likes solving problems, so it can be natural for people to get into analysis when they should be focusing on restoring service.

Do not hold incidents open to do root cause analysis when service is already restored. Incident records should be closed and problem records raised correctly. This practice is bad for incident metrics, if nothing else.

Be wary of 'post-incident reviews', which are often problem management in disguise. Get problem management in place instead and do not allow support teams to do post-incident review and then hand over the resolution to problem management to project manage.

PROACTIVE PROBLEM MANAGEMENT

Proactive problem management is the other path into the problem management process. Proactive problem management is essentially an analysis process, looking at all sources of information available that could highlight potential or actual problems in the environment, other than problems highlighted directly by individual incidents that have occurred. I define the environment broadly to include applications, infrastructure, processes, people, vendors and everything else involved in delivering IT services. At least some of an organisation's efforts should be directed to analysis and review, to uncover such potential problems.

Make time for proactive problem management. If possible, ensure that at least one problem manager is dedicated full-time to proactive problem management. Alternatively, if the only staff available is a process owner for problem management who is not directly involved in reactive problem investigations, they should allocate 80 per cent of their time to analysis and looking for potential problems. Only 20 per cent of their time should be given to administration, standards' adherence and other activities.

Importantly, once raised, proactive and reactive problems follow exactly the same path through investigation, error resolution, review and closure. The process for dealing with problems is the same, it is just the detection process that is different.

Sources of information that might point to potential problems are quite varied, but they generally fall into three categories:

- process outputs;
- people;
- data analysis.

While these categories are not clear-cut and will overlap, they help to organise the discussion.

Process outputs

Several service management processes can include steps that identify potential problems. Process outputs can be inputs to further analysis, but they can also indicate problems directly. Incident, knowledge, change, release and problem management itself all fit into this latter category. Capacity management, event management, availability management and service level management do as well; however, their outputs are more likely to be data that points to potential problems and so they are discussed below under data analysis.

Near misses are a rich source of potential problems for investigation. A near miss is simply a situation where a process has almost failed, but has been put back into kilter by an intervention. Many operational 'workarounds' mask underlying problems. An example is an invoice processing system that identifies an invoice with incorrect or missing customer code and puts it into a special queue for operator attention. The volume and types of manual intervention might indicate an underlying problem somewhere in the invoicing or ordering process.

Other types of near miss are those in the 'lucky timing' category, an incident that could have been a major service interruption, but was low impact because of the time of day or day of the week when it happened. These types of incidents should raise concerns because they might happen again at a more unfortunate time, thereby causing a significant loss or impacting a customer to a greater degree.

Project and release post-implementation reviews can be a source of proactive problems, either in the conduct of the project or in its deliverables, particularly if there were scope changes or cuts during implementation. There might be potential problems that are created from incomplete implementation of project deliverables, poor or incorrect documentation, releases that include known application faults, or lack of proper handover of new services to operations support teams. Generally, project managers will highlight their successful deliverables and many will be happy to point out where there were shortcomings, while some will be less open about problems they know about. Examining the project risk register might reveal unresolved problems.

The same rules around trust and assigning no blame apply to projects and releases as they do to support activities. If reporting problems is seen as positive, it is more likely to occur.

As discussed in Chapter 6, problem management can generate new problem investigations during existing investigations, especially where it appears that a combination of factors or events led to an incident. While reactive problem management investigates and resolves the main or primary root cause, events such as contributing factors might also need to be addressed. Are such problems proactive or reactive? Again, pragmatically speaking, it does not matter, as long as the problems are addressed.

The Kepner–Tregoe methodology formalises an additional extension of problem management into what it calls 'extend the cause, extend the fix'. Simply put, when a root cause is found, this means considering what other types of incident this problem might also cause and addressing those as well. Similarly, when a solution is being implemented, consider what other problems this fix might also address, in other systems, locations or business areas. Proactive problems can be raised to track these additional implementations.

Risk management and problem management are very closely related. In fact it can be argued that problem management is a subcategory of operational risk management. Risks that need to be addressed can be raised as proactive problems and the risk register can be viewed as a list of unresolved problems. In addition, a deferred problem is another representation of a known, but unresolved, risk.

FMEA is a common risk assessment methodology that I have also seen used as a proactive problem management tool.

Knowledge management is discussed again under data analysis, but I want to mention an observation from a former colleague, David Ireland. He noted that by reviewing knowledge articles used frequently to resolve incidents, it is possible for service desk and knowledge management teams to suggest problems that need preventative solutions, thus leading to proactive problem investigations.

People

People in other service delivery teams, client managers, operations and support teams, even the CEO or CIO having conversations with colleagues and customers, can raise potential problems that might need to be investigated. They should be able to use a request process to suggest problems to the PAB for evaluation.

Knowledgeable people have hunches, which are intuitions that work at the intersection of knowledge and unconscious processing and are quite different from guesswork. Hunches are a rich source of potential problems and should be taken seriously. An example is an engineer who sees an event, remembers that something similar has happened before and that it might suggest that there is an underlying issue in the IT environment. You should record hunches from both technical staff and from customers.

It is important to act on hunches that have been raised. They should be investigated to verify if there is something in them. Either take appropriate action or give reasons why not. It is probably obvious that if issues raised as potential problems through the intuition of technical staff or the impressions of customers seem to fall on deaf ears, the credibility of problem management will be eroded and a source of intelligence about potential problems will probably be lost. People will naturally think 'Why raise something if nothing will be done about it?'

David Ireland also found that manual errors are potential problems. He recommends engaging with business operations staff to find manual activities, assess the risk and then automate high-risk activities to solve potential problems proactively. Equally, this approach can be applied to manual processes in IT service delivery.

Every engagement with clients should be seen as an opportunity for finding problems proactively. Identify upcoming events in the business calendar and look at patterns of business activity to understand where clients think problems might arise in the near future.

Lastly, I group vendors in the people category. They can suggest preventative actions that need to be considered, including patches and forthcoming changes to functionality. Most vendors also have user groups and forums, where the experiences of other customers with the product might suggest potential problems for investigation.

Data analysis

All IT service organisations have a wealth of data available. How successful you are in taking an analytical approach to detecting problems depends on your organisation's attitude to data and your team's skills. I think most of the analysis required to find problems proactively is not overly complex and can be adopted by almost any team.

Pattern and trend analysis are two basic data analysis techniques that are useful for finding problems proactively. Pattern analysis is about looking for how data is arranged: for example observing the distribution of existing root causes into categories, or that certain events always happen on Mondays. Trends are a special sort of pattern, where direction is the key attribute. Individual facts or occurrences change their meaning depending on the direction (or absence) of a trend. Trends are usually an increase or decrease in a value, or the approach to a predefined threshold or limit.

Patterns are typically found by grouping data by category. This could be symptom data from incidents, or incidents occurring by application, by support group or by geographical location. Problem cause data is often analysed using Pareto analysis, which I will cover separately below. However, you will also recall the examples that I gave in Chapter 7 regarding problem causes. This simple type of analysis can very quickly indicate where proactive problem investigations can deliver immediate improvements. For example, if you can group your existing problems by cause type and relate them to specific applications, you might be able to show that a particular development team has a poor approach to testing that has led to repeated stability issues.

A common statistical method when analysing data is to discard 'outliers' – records that are well away from the norm. When analysing potential sources of problems, outliers are very valuable and should always be examined. For example, if a particular batch process normally takes between 30 minutes and one hour, but once each month it runs for more than two hours, rather than ignore these unusual runs, they should be investigated in detail to understand what is actually going on. Anomalies can often point to problems that might suddenly cause a major incident.

Trends and patterns do not come only from problem management data, of course. Service desks commonly review their call data and statistics. I mentioned earlier that an analysis of the utilisation of knowledge articles might reveal highly utilised articles, which could be pointing to repeating incidents that should be investigated. SLA breaches or near breaches can also point to problems that need investigating. An example of a worrying trend is an availability statistic that is creeping closer to agreed thresholds, or going from green to amber.

Most environments have thresholds, and it is the ones that are getting close to acceptable limits that can prompt proactive problem management. This is where problem management overlaps with capacity management, service level management and availability management.

The idea of tracking thresholds is about catching and fixing problems that are creeping up on us, or systems that are running almost at their limits. An example I was told about was a batch that ran almost right up to the deadline. The customer did not care, unless the report was not available at 4 a.m. If the batch finished at 3.59 a.m., all was well. The run time was getting closer and closer to 4 a.m., so a proactive problem was raised to understand why the times were getting longer, and the cause was found and a fix applied. The job now finishes every night with several hours to spare. Problem management is a sensible way of capturing and dealing with this type of trending issue.

Pareto analysis

A short 'how-to' guide to Pareto analysis is included here for completeness because it is a very useful technique that all problem managers should be able to use. This guide is mainly drawn from two books: *The Lean Six Sigma Pocket Toolbook* (George *et al.*, 2005) and *Making Sense of Data* (Wheeler, 2003). As well as Pareto analysis, each of these books contains a wealth of other data analysis tools and techniques. Although aimed at process management and improvement, the tools they talk about can make a big impact on the quality of service delivery in general and problem analysis in particular.

Often referred to as the '80–20 rule', Pareto analysis aims to get a consensus about where to focus one's efforts. The analysis method is based on categorising data (in our case, problems, causes, incidents, and so on) in an attempt to highlight which categories cover the bulk of the cases. A bar chart is constructed from the categories, which is overlaid by a line chart of the cumulative total. Figure 11.1 is an example.

The visual representation of the data is useful for two reasons. Firstly, as in the example, it quickly shows what is having the biggest impact (where incidents are coming from) and makes communication of the issues much simpler. In this way, a Pareto chart:

- can break a big problem into smaller pieces;
- quickly identify the most significant factors;
- show where to focus effort; and
- allow better use of limited resources.

Figure 11.1 Pareto analysis of sales system incidents

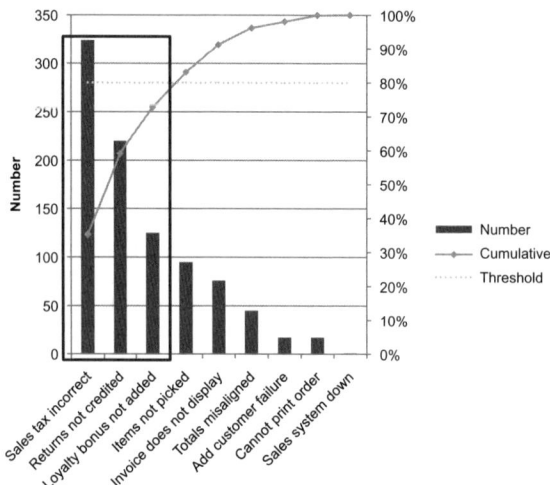

Secondly, if it takes most of the categories to get to 80 per cent, then this indicates that there is a more fundamental issue that needs investigation. Wheeler (2003, pp.46–52) calls this a flat Pareto chart, which points to 'across the board' problems in processes. George et al. (2005, p.144) note that in this case, it can be valuable to look at problems that might be affecting all categories.

The most frequent incidents might not have the biggest impact. Recutting the data based on impact (cost, time to resolve, business disruption) might give a better idea of which problems to attack first (George et al., 2005, p.144).

The main success factor in Pareto analysis is the selection of the categories for analysis. Like any statistical method, the choice of what data to analyse is the key to the quality of the analysis. Many teams assess incident impact and frequency data to highlight areas that might need special attention, such as a particular application or part of the infrastructure, or a particular time of the day, week or month. In one case, I used Pareto analysis to show that more incidents were coming from legacy applications than new releases, counter to the general assumption that poorly tested new applications were the biggest source of instability for customers. Pareto analysis of incident data, therefore, is a very useful exercise and should be part of the fundamental activity of any problem management team.

An equally effective pool of data for problem management is confirmed root causes. This is where real and often unexpected benefit can be found. By looking at the pattern of causes, deeper underlying problems can be revealed. I discussed change as a root cause in Chapter 6. I used Pareto analysis on cause data to show that it was not the change management process itself that was the cause. Change management, after all, is just a conduit to manage the introduction of new things into the environment. It was the lack of adequate testing by application development teams that was causing the incidents. Although a general problem, the analysis clearly showed that some groups were worse than others, leading to a drive to improve testing overall, while first targeting those areas that would make the biggest difference. The eventual result was a significant improvement in the stability of several key applications.

The Further reading section provides links to several websites with more information on Pareto analysis, including the Chandoo website that explains very clearly how to use Microsoft® Excel® to produce the necessary charts.

LOGGING PROBLEMS

Every problem detected or proposed, whether reactive or proactive, should be logged, before any decisions are made about what to do about it. It is important that problems are not 'lost'. The reasons why a problem will not be investigated should be recorded in the problem record. In this way you can track what happened to them, which is important in managing stakeholder expectations.

It is therefore sensible to have a decision point in the process to make sure that only valid problems are investigated. This assessment forms the next step in the process.

12 ASSESS, PRIORITISE AND ASSIGN PROBLEMS

Table 12.1 Assess, prioritise and assign states and metrics

Incoming state	New
Incoming sub-states	None
Who is involved	Problem manager, PAB, IT management
Outgoing state	Assigned or Root cause analysis, Error resolution, Ready for review
Outgoing sub-states	(Ready for review:) Duplicate, Rejected
Time stamps	Problem created date, set to Assigned, set to Root cause analysis, set to Error resolution
Relevant metrics	Days in new status
Calculations	Assigned or Root cause analysis time stamp minus Problem created time stamp

ASSESS THE PROBLEM

Investigating every problem logged should not be automatic. Assess every problem logged to make sure it is worth investigating.

Not all incidents lead to problem management. Especially early in the adoption and maturity of problem management, there can be pressure to raise a problem for every incident, so that there is always a one-to-one relationship. This is not the most effective and efficient way to approach problem management. Often, many incidents display the same symptoms, suggesting a possible common cause. A single problem investigation usually solves multiple incidents.

The first check on a newly logged problem is whether there is already a problem investigation in progress. If so, mark the new one as a duplicate and send it for review and closure. Make sure that any incident records linked to the duplicate problem are connected to the actual problem.

If the prioritisation step discussed next results in a very low priority problem, I would reject it as well. It probably will not be investigated and it represents a very low operational risk. I would argue that it has been raised in error.

Some of the frameworks discussed in Chapter 13 suggest that you only open a problem if you do not know the root cause. In reality, you will have situations where the cause was found in the incident investigation, but a permanent solution was not. I raise a problem in these cases and set the state to error resolution, skipping over the root cause analysis phase. The assigned problem manager is then responsible for finding and implementing the solution, as well as any additional follow-up actions that arose during the incident.

You might like to consider requiring the problem manager to double-check the validity of the cause. This might be useful early in the implementation of problem management.

The last assessment I recommend is the concept of a control barrier. It is usually not possible to manage a cause that is outside the organisation's control – for example, how a purchased software package or an upstream supplier's service, such as a communications carrier network, works internally. This also applies to government and other regulated services. There is no advantage in attempting a problem investigation, which intends to find and fix the errors. When the cause is outside your control, all that should be done is to review the risks, use what influence you can with the vendor or supplier to fix issues and implement mitigating controls to protect the organisation against failures.

Decide the limits of your organisation's control and treat problems beyond the barrier as risk mitigation exercises.

CATEGORISATION

ITIL® puts a categorisation step in the process here (Cabinet Office, 2011, pp.102–103). While it can be useful to categorise incidents before investigation, I believe that this step is misplaced in the problem management process flow. In practice, problems are categorised by their root causes, which can only occur after the root cause investigation. Any categorisation now would likely need to change once the true cause is known.

I think that, often, early categorisation is done to assign the problem to a particular technical or support group for investigation. For example, an incident that is blamed on the network might be assigned to the networks team. I have never seen this work as intended, unless problem management is mature and everyone has been well trained. Once a problem is assigned to an SME team, they typically do enough investigation to 'prove' it is not their problem. You can see what happens. Problems are passed around, no one takes ownership, and either a lot of time is wasted before a proper investigation uncovers the cause or nothing gets resolved.

Clearly, this is unsatisfactory. Remember the statistic I quoted in Chapter 6, that about two-thirds of all 'causes' assumed during incident investigations were wrong. This means that early categorisation will also be wrong in these cases. Instead, make sure a problem manager owns the problem and conducts a structured investigation including all the relevant SMEs at the start.

Only categorise problems once the root cause is known. If you cannot find the root cause, the 'category' will be 'unknown'. Many tools include category fields. Simply fill them out later in the process, not at the start.

PRIORITISATION

Prioritisation drives the selection of which problems to investigate. Deciding what to investigate will always be a trade-off between the cost of the investigation and the impact and risk of an actual or potential incident. Ranking problems ensures the best use of limited resources. Problem prioritisation ensures that the most important problems get the necessary attention and resources to solve them.

Incident severity is the primary driver of priority. It works for both reactive and proactive problems. In Figure 12.1, P1 means priority one and so on.

Figure 12.1 Primary problem prioritisation

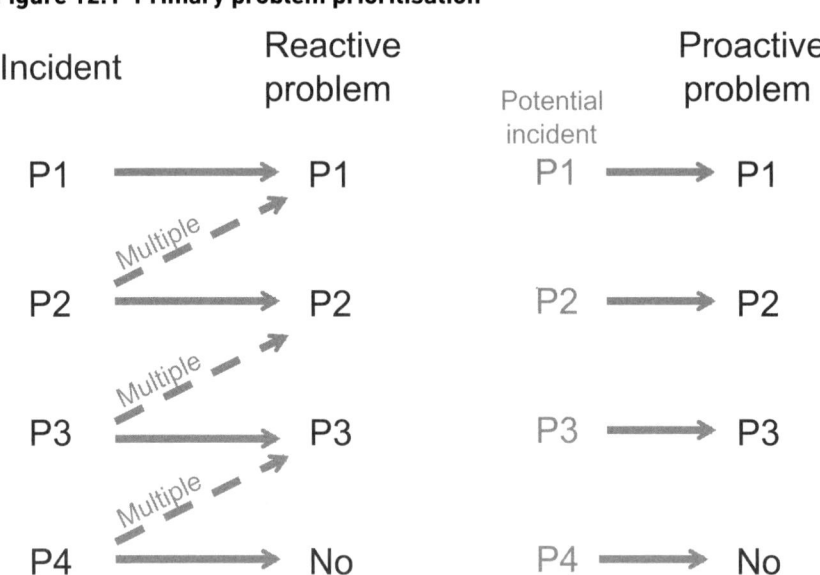

For a reactive problem, the priority is at least as high as the incident it investigates.

• Multiple incidents or recurring incidents can push up the priority of the problem investigation. For example, several P2 incidents might prompt a P1 problem and several P3 incidents might trigger a P2.

- Problems can jump priorities – a flood of P4 incidents could conceivably raise a P2 problem.
- Limitations on resources means that P4 incidents should not trigger problems individually.

For a proactive problem, assess priority by the risk of occurrence, potential impact and urgency of potential incidents.

- Generally, the priority of the potential incidents drives the priority of the problem investigation.
- As with reactive problems, resource limitations preclude low priority proactive problem investigations.

The point here is 'de-coupling'. The priority of a problem can be different from the severity of an incident, simply because one problem raised to investigate multiple incidents would very likely have a higher priority than the individual repeating incidents. Repeating or similar incidents generally point to a bigger problem, so it follows that the investigation should be prioritised accordingly.

If your organisation seems to be confused about the difference between incidents and problems, you might want to consider using a different naming convention for problem priorities. Incidents could be severity 1, 2 and 3, for instance, while problems could priority 1, 2 and 3, or high, medium and low. I have used both approaches and I found that having a different naming convention helped. The approach you take will depend on which one causes the least confusion in your organisation.

In many implementations, this simple approach to setting priority is all that is done. However, I find that there needs to be a mechanism to provide management input into priorities and to add granularity, to make priority more accurate.

At the very least the PAB, or other governance methods you have adopted, should have a say in setting priority. This can provide the relationship to the overall objectives and priorities of the organisation, to target problems that are having a direct negative impact on objectives. It also helps to prevent setting problem priority in isolation within the problem management team.

Management always wants input into work priorities. Problem management is no exception.

With a single level priority scheme, it is quite common to have multiple problems with the same priority. It is challenging to know which ones to work on first. A criteria matrix can be used to set problem priority in a repeatable and consistent way, so that the most serious problems are given the greatest attention in the work queue. Table 12.2 gives an example.

Table 12.2 A sample criteria matrix

Criteria	Value
Severity 1 incident	50
Severity 2 incident	25
Business or management priority	25
Pareto top 20	25
Potential threat to business cycle	15
Severity 3 incident	10
Commonly used technology	10
Incidents for one system greater than 50	10
Repeat or multiple recent incidents	5
Cause unknown	5
Incidents for one system 10 to 50	5
Severity 4 incident	1
Incidents for one system less than 10	1

A problem can have several factors influencing priority at once, so it is OK to pick multiple criteria. For example repeat or multiple severity 2 incidents, where the cause is unknown and there is a threat to a process that is required for an important event in the business cycle, would score 50.

The accumulated score is then used to select the priority. In the example, a score of 50 means it is a priority one problem. The selection boundaries are set so that the guarantees for primary prioritisation are automatically achieved. A severity 2 incident will always be investigated as at least a priority 2 problem (Table 12.3).

Table 12.3 A priority scoring matrix

Problem priority	Minimum	Maximum
Priority 1	50	N/A
Priority 2	25	49
Priority 3	10	24
Not for investigation	1	9

These matrices can be used manually, during incident handover or afterwards during the PAB meeting. They can also be included in your toolset, as a set of checkboxes, with the calculations happening in the background.

There are several benefits to this approach. It removes guesswork and introduces consistency. It allows value judgements in a controlled manner, while countering the effects of politics. Management can also see that their input is taken into account and that business priorities flow through appropriately. Lastly, if the final scores are made visible, it is possible to rank problems of the same overall priority against each other.

If you want proactive problems to have a higher priority, add a criterion for 'proactive' and give it a value sufficient to push proactive problems up the priority list.

If you want to know more about risks and prioritisation, the Mind Tools® website has some good material, open to all (www.mindtools.com). It includes an impact probability worksheet that you might find useful. I have included the link in the references.

ASSIGNMENT

The last step before root cause analysis begins is to assign the problem to a problem manager. Depending on the model you have adopted, this will be a problem manager dedicated to a specific area, assigned from a central pool according to workload balance, or assigned in accordance with the required experience and seniority, depending on the priority.

Accountability for problems was discussed in Section 2. Although there needs to be a mechanism for passing problems from one accountable person to another, this should be avoided if possible. A common approach I have seen is to change the assignment of the problem, as opinions about possible causes change, or the problem moves from investigation to resolution. Many of the practitioners interviewed for this book think that this is a bad idea and that accountability should stay with one problem manager throughout its life. This means that assignment should not change unless under exceptional circumstances.

13 INVESTIGATION AND DIAGNOSIS

Table 13.1 Investigation and diagnosis states and metrics

Incoming state	Assigned or Root cause analysis
Incoming sub-states	None
Who is involved	SMEs, problem manager
Outgoing state	Error resolution, Ready for review
Outgoing sub-states	(Error resolution:) Investigate solution, (Ready for review:) Root cause not found
Time stamps	Set to Root cause analysis, set to Error resolution, set to Ready for review
Relevant metrics	Days to find root cause, percentage of root causes found
Calculations	Error resolution minus Assigned or Root cause analysis, Ready for review minus Assigned or Root cause analysis (if root cause not found)

This step of the process aims to find the cause of the problem. It is commonly referred to as root cause analysis or RCA. Almost every source I have reviewed states that RCA is a step-by-step, structured method that leads to the discovery of a fault's first or 'root' cause.

I have been talking about a structured approach throughout this book, particularly in Chapter 5, and I will not revisit this material. Instead, I will talk quickly about the psychology behind the need for structure and then summarise the main structured approaches I have encountered.

Kahnemann (2012) has found that leaping to conclusions is inbuilt in all of us. Humans 'apply causal thinking inappropriately' and assume causality, even when it is not there (pp.76–77). While mental shortcuts are automatic and very useful, perhaps even a survival adaptation, problem-solving requires a conscious effort to step away from that type of thinking and engage the analytical system directly. This is why structured methods are important, to 'avoid jumping to cause', as Kepner–Tregoe put it in their training materials (Kepner–Tregoe, 2010, p.3-1).

Dietrich Dörner wrote an interesting book on the errors we make in complex situations. He notes that we have a tendency to make incorrect assumptions and, once made, defend false assumptions quite strongly (Dörner, 1996, p.42). I often see this tendency in problem investigations and it is another reason why applying a structured method is valuable.

Define the problem precisely before trying to solve it.

Without a clear statement of the problem, analysis will be a struggle at best, or will, at worst, solve the wrong problem. Attempts to solve multiple problems simultaneously almost always fail. Similarly, this is seen in root causes. A woolly root cause that does not seem to fully address the problem points to a poorly defined problem statement.

Some of the following structured methods are just about problem analysis, some are about risk analysis and some cover the whole process from cause to implemented fix. Several of the 'whole process' methods cannibalise other methods for their actual analysis stage.

MAJOR INVESTIGATION FRAMEWORKS

Kepner–Tregoe

Kepner–Tregoe is a consulting and training company that owns and delivers the KT methodology. KT is an approach to problem-solving and decision-making that encompasses situational appraisal, decision analysis and potential problem analysis, as well as the problem analysis component specific to finding the cause of problems. It applies a rigorous structure to describing the problem, identifying possible causes, evaluating possible causes and confirming the true cause. Their approach is the one most often 'borrowed' by other methods, sometimes without acknowledgement. It works best if you do their KT training, which leads to better outcomes than just reading their book (*The New Rational Manager*) and attempting to apply the techniques from there. I have used this method extensively and find it to be very effective.

KEPNERandFOURIE

Dr Kepner separated from KT several years ago and developed the framework in a different direction. I will not try to compare the two or state a preference, except to say that KEPNERandFOURIE is more tailored to IT than KT. It is the framework I currently use. Thinking Dimensions supplied this definition:

KEPNERandFOURIE is a structured IT root cause analysis methodology specially designed and developed by Dr Chuck Kepner and Dr Matthys Fourie for the IT industry (both of whom still develop IP for IT and business with Thinking Dimensions Global). This IT root cause analysis methodology is a combination of factual information gathered during the information gathering phase coupled with the intuition of the appropriate SME's to achieve both accuracy and speed with any incident and problem investigation. Applicable to all disciplines within the IT industry.

Thinking Dimensions Global is the global sole distributor of the KEPNERandFOURIE™ Thinking Technology.

Eight Disciplines

Eight Disciplines (8D) is one of the problem-solving frameworks that covers the whole process. Originally formulated by the Ford Motor Company, it is exactly what it says: a set of eight 'disciplines' that represent the steps in the process of finding and fixing problems. It has an industrial orientation rather than an IT flavour. It does not specifically include a root cause analysis technique; instead it references other established methods. I particularly like discipline eight, 'celebrate success with the team'.

It is not a framework I have used, but I have included references to Mind Tools® and an ebook by Carter for those who want to know more.

TapRooT®

This approach to problem-solving is particularly strong in assessing human factors and is applied widely in industry. Like most frameworks, it is not specifically oriented to IT problem-solving. This short summary is from their website.

The TapRooT® System is a 7-step investigation process with built-in tools that help an investigator like you:

- collect information;
- understand what happened;
- identify the problems that caused the incident;
- analyse each problem's root causes;
- look beyond root causes for systemic, cultural and organisational factors;
- develop fixes to improve performance and stop repeat incidents;
- present what's been learned to management so they can understand and approve the fixes.

I think it is a system that deserves consideration when assessing problem-solving techniques (see also Paradies and Ungar, 2008).

Fault tree analysis

Fault tree analysis is a visual approach to creating hierarchies of conditions, events and barriers in an 'event and causal factor tree'. It is often applied to systems before they fail, as a proactive technique for risk analysis, asking what could go wrong and how to prevent it. However, it is applied to root cause analysis after the event as well. The quite well-known NASA Root cause analysis overview is a very good example of how to use the technique and apply it to root cause analysis. It is well worth having this technique in your repertoire, particularly if you find visual approaches useful. The NASA overview is also worth reading as an excellent general introduction to root cause analysis.

Failure mode and effects analysis

The FMEA technique was originally developed for improving safety in the aerospace industry. It aims to identify faults before they occur. One of the most useful contributions of FMEA is the idea of calculating a risk priority number for each effect or failure mode, which can be applied directly to prioritising proactive problems. Drawing on *The Basics of FMEA* (McDermott, Mikulak and Beauregard, 2009, p.23), the ten steps are:

1. Review the process or product.
2. Brainstorm potential failure modes.
3. List potential effects of each failure mode.
4. Assign a severity ranking for each effect.
5. Assign an occurrence ranking for each failure mode.
6. Assign a detection ranking for each failure mode and/or effect.
7. Calculate the risk priority number (RPN) of each effect.
8. Prioritise the failure modes for action.
9. Take action to eliminate or reduce the high-risk failure modes.
10. Calculate the resulting RPN as the failure modes are reduced or eliminated.

This risk management approach is something that IT organisations could easily apply through proactive problem management.

SUPPORTING INVESTIGATION TOOLS

Five Whys and other question and answer techniques

Five Whys is widely noted as a root cause analysis methodology. It is not. It is a short-hand description of the more general question and answer techniques that are included in most frameworks, for example, 'questioning to the void' from KT and KEPNERandFOURIE. It is often stated that you should get to root cause by the fifth question. The limitation is that two different people will often get through two completely different sets of five questions from the same starting point and arrive at different conclusions. The weaknesses of Five Whys are discussed in two web articles included in the references, one from the *Quality Digest* by Stewart Anderson and one from Workplace Psychology.

However, it is useful as a test to make sure you really have a root cause and there is not something else behind it. If you cannot answer why, you can be pretty sure you are at the end of the chain.

Ishikawa diagrams

Kaoru Ishikawa was a practitioner in the quality movement. The diagrams that bear his name are also called 'fishbone diagrams' because they look like a fish skeleton. They are related to both brainstorming and failure mode analysis as a method of organising results into a visual display that helps understand the results. While very useful for problem analysis, Ishikawa diagrams are not a specific problem-solving tool; rather they are a general tool for organising information visually. Like Five Whys, they are often mentioned as a problem-solving framework, but this is a misunderstanding of their purpose.

Ishikawa diagrams, because they are visual, are suitable for face-to-face problem-solving, but harder to use in a distributed organisation, where many problem investigations are managed via teleconference. Even so, I do know people who use them very effectively remotely to organise the group's thinking and either distribute it later or share it online.

Brainstorming and mind mapping

This is a technique that I use frequently in many contexts. It is very useful to generate a list of possible causes for a problem. The basic idea is to use a Mind Map® (a trademark of the Buzan Organisation) to capture ideas as they are generated. There are many references to brainstorming available, including the Mind Tools® website mentioned in the references. The key factor is to suspend judgement, and to just get the information down and not try to edit it as you go. There are similar steps in KT and KEPNERandFOURIE. It takes practice, but I think the ability to lead a brainstorming session is a necessary skill for all problem managers.

Rapid problem resolution

Rapid problem resolution (RPR) is an approach to diagnosing technical problems (Offord, 2011). The organisation behind it, Advance 7, recommends it as a technique to pursue when other techniques have not yielded results. It depends on capturing symptoms and underlying event data, matching them up to reveal underlying causes. While I have not used it myself, it has a solid following in the UK as an approach to technology-based problems. It fits well into a scenario where the root cause has not been found, the problem is pending and additional data capture tools have been deployed while waiting for a recurrence of the incident.

Pareto analysis

Pareto analysis is a data analysis technique that is useful to sort out which problems to investigate. I covered it in Chapter 11. While it helps you focus on which problems, if solved, will yield the biggest results, I do not see it as a root cause analysis tool.

Pain value analysis

This is a prioritisation technique that assesses impact in order to choose which problems to investigate and solve. It is another technique that is sometimes incorrectly noted as a root cause analysis technique, when it clearly is not.

Crowd sourcing and asking others

A technique for problem-solving that has been made more effective by modern technology is to simply ask others, expert or not, what the cause of your problem might be. Crowd sourcing has proved to be a very useful adjunct tool for problem managers. Service desks and technical support teams already use a form of crowd sourcing extensively. Most engineers are familiar with accessing internal or vendor knowledge bases to solve problems. Many will routinely use Google to look up error messages instead of paid-for support databases.

I think it is a valid tool to extend the reach of problem management when looking for possible causes as well as solutions. Used critically, it can add an outsider view that might not otherwise be available to small organisations.

Collaboration tools

Many tools for root cause analysis rely on being in one room. This is not often practical in larger organisations where people are dispersed geographically and often across time zones. Analysis can typically be carried out via teleconference for at least some of the participants. In these situations, a few modifications are warranted or different tools are required.

The most obvious is for the problem manager chairing the meeting to share his or her desktop via a tool such as Cisco WebEx or GoToMeeting from Citrix. This means drawing and listing tools can then be viewed by all, for such tasks as sharing a system diagram or organising or rearranging the timeline of events.

There are many other tools available, and support for collaboration is also being incorporated into major service management toolsets.

OTHER DEFINITIONS OF PROBLEM, PROBLEM MANAGEMENT, ROOT CAUSE ANALYSIS

I talked in earlier chapters about how problem management is a discipline that is not restricted to IT. Most of the frameworks mentioned above were not founded with IT in mind; they are generalised problem-solving approaches. I recommend that problem managers review the many methodologies available from quality assurance, complex system and safety analysis, human performance enhancement and general business management fields for fresh ideas and approaches to problem-solving. I have included several useful books in the references and Further reading section.

ROOT CAUSE QUALITY: GETTING TO 'REAL' ROOT CAUSES

I often see root cause statements that are all about what happened, but not why. It is simply a restatement of the facts of the incident, for example, 'The implementer made a cut and paste error on the command line.' This is a statement of what happened, but why did that cause the incident?

Questioning techniques are very useful to confirm root cause. Simply put, if you can ask why and get an answer, you have not reached the true root cause. In the example above, a series of questions that started with 'How did this cause the incident?' led to 'The change instructions were not well defined, scripted and tested before implementation. The post implementation checks were not adequate to test full functionality after the change.' This was the real root cause.

Of course, you can go too far with open-ended questions, so the ultimate test is: If we apply a solution to address this cause, will it prevent future incidents of this type? If the answer is yes, then, on the balance of probabilities and pragmatically, this is the root cause.

Finding the real root cause leads to implementing the correct error resolution, which is the next step in the process.

14 ERROR RESOLUTION

Table 14.1 Error resolution states and metrics

Incoming state	Error resolution
Incoming sub-states	Investigate solution
Who is involved	SMEs, problem manager, PAB, financial management
Outgoing state	Ready for review
Outgoing sub-states	Solution not found, Solution not approved, Ready for closure
Time stamps	Set to Error resolution, set to Solution approved, set to Ready for review
Relevant metrics	Days to find and approve solution, Days to implement solution
Calculations	Solution approved minus Error resolution time stamp, Ready for review minus Solution implemented time stamp

The error resolution process covers all activities linked to the implementation of a sustainable resolution for an error, which, as noted earlier, is the ITIL® definition ('known error') for a problem once its cause is known.

This stage could just as easily be called 'problem resolution' because the introduction of the additional term 'error' seems unnecessary to me.

New problems can come straight to this stage, skipping root cause analysis, if the root cause is already known. Remember that problems still have to be fixed, so this is more effective than assuming that, if the cause is known, problem management is not required.

I discussed who owns this part of the process in Chapter 5. Although SMEs have the responsibility to find and implement solutions, the problem manager, or the problem management process itself, needs to ensure that there is proper engagement, prioritisation, timely approval, progress reporting and, where necessary, escalation to address delays and failures.

ITIL® covers error resolution mainly as handling known error records and raising a change request (Cabinet Office, 2011, p.105). While it is true that one or more change requests might be required, there is a lot more to it than just raising a change. Error resolution is a joint initiative between problem managers and SMEs such as system architects, application developers and infrastructure engineers, as well as the relevant service manager, financial management, the customer and other stakeholders. Depending on the size of the issue, it can be a single step or a major exercise, including:

- assessing the options available to fix the error;
- costing and proposing the most appropriate solution;
- presenting to management for approval; and then
- scheduling the solution for implementation.

These are the four distinct phases or sub-processes, which all problems go through when resolving errors.

FIND A SOLUTION

Sometimes the way to fix a problem is obvious. For example, it might clearly be an application processing error, which needs a coding change. Most problems, however, might need some investigation to establish the best solution. Occasionally, no solution appears possible, which I rarely find to be the case. This is why 'solution not approved' is more common than 'solution not found'. In almost all cases, something can be done to fix a problem.

I find that brainstorming is just as useful to find potential solutions as it is to find possible causes. In general, the SME teams will come up with the solutions, but it can be a very effective use of a problem manager's time to run a short brainstorming session with them, to make sure a range of options are actually considered. Too often, an SME team left to itself will come up with a solution that suits them when a better solution might be available. What they propose in isolation might be the easiest, the most interesting solution to deploy, or it might achieve something else they want at the same time. You need to know about all of the available options before deciding what to do.

Do not overlook non-technical solutions. Sometimes a simple process change, such as an approval step or a checklist, can be just as effective as a technical safeguard or preventative measure.

Gather a range of options and use a decision matrix to pick the best option. Several of the problem-solving frameworks also include effective approaches to decision-making.

In the unlikely event that a solution cannot be found, the problem should be set to 'ready for review' and marked as 'solution not found'. Your governance process should then have the opportunity to review the problem and perhaps ask for another attempt to find a solution, escalate to a more senior problem manager or deeper-level technical team, or call on vendor assistance. The alternative is to defer the problem, though it is probably better to find a solution instead.

The number of problems deferred with no solution should be tracked because if the number seems excessive, it might indicate that there is something wrong with your process. Finding solutions is a key factor in the success of problem management.

THE SOLUTION PROPOSAL

The development of a solution proposal might not be an obvious step to take. However, it is a good discipline to adopt because it forces problem managers to ensure that solutions are assessed properly. Even with a single, obvious solution, it is necessary to compare the solution, its costs and its resource requirements against the 'do nothing' option, as well against for what other purposes that budget could be used. Remember that doing nothing continues to incur the cost of recurring incidents; it is not a zero-cost option.

> Use whatever is the standard way of presenting requests for budget and resources in your organisation. If the solution is a major piece of work to implement, you might need a formal project initiation proposal – prepared by a project manager and not the problem manager.

There are several essential requirements to cover:

- A restatement of the problem and its business impact, preferably including the cost impact of ongoing incidents.

- A summary of the urgency of the solution requirement, perhaps highlighting pending business events, such as a major sales initiative or a busy period, that further incidents could disrupt.

- Based on the impact of the problem and the urgency of the required solution, an assessment of the priority of the proposal. This is important because it allows the approving body to compare the request against other contending pieces of work.

- A short description of the solution proposed, the staff and budget required, the expected time needed to implement it, the risk that the solution will not address the problem and how you are going to test that it has worked.

- A short summary of the other options considered and why each was discarded. Depending on your organisation, you might have to start the proposal with this list, though it is better to leave it until later in the proposal if possible.

- A request for approval, budget and resource allocation and confirmation of the timetable for implementation.

APPROVAL

I think it should be mandatory to include and enforce an approval step in any error resolution process. Fixing problems takes time and money and, in most organisations, problem management does not have its own budget and resources to allocate to implementing solutions, which means problems have to be fixed from funds and resources allocated from other teams. Approval commits the organisation to implementing the solution in an agreed time-frame and ensures that:

- resources are planned and allocated before execution;
- the solution is compliant with the organisation's architectural standards;
- a risk/cost/benefit assessment has been done; and
- all parties agree to proceed as scheduled.

Not all proposals will be approved. Some will be too expensive compared with the cost of living with the problem. Others might be judged to be not required because the application or platform is to be retired or to be changed significantly in the near future. As discussed in Chapter 15, these problems should be sent for review by the governing body to decide what to do.

Only implement approved solutions. Problem management is usually not in a position to decide what fixes to implement.

IMPLEMENTATION

In almost all situations, problem managers are not the implementers of the solution. They remain accountable, but SMEs are responsible for putting the fix into production. The role of the problem manager is to track and monitor the implementation, then to review and confirm that the solution has fixed the problem.

This part of the process is one of two major bottlenecks in problem management (the other is taking on problems, particularly from incident management, which I covered in Chapter 11). Failure to drive an effective resolution process is probably the most common source of failure for problem management. The length of time it takes to get problems fixed often has a negative impact on the overall performance of the process. The main reason is competing priorities for resources in the SME teams themselves.

Sometimes, management does not have a clear method for assigning projects, tasks and day-to-day support work in a way that make priorities clear for team members. The unintended result is that they leave it up to individuals to choose what they work on. At other times, problem solutions are not given an equal or higher importance as projects or general support work. Finally, some teams are rewarded for implementing new solutions but not for improving stability by fixing problems. The only solution to these issues is effective tracking and reporting by the problem managers, good governance and ensuring that development and operations managers understand the importance of stability and fixing problems. Once again, the PAB is a suitable body to set and drive priorities by approving solutions for implementation and allocating resources to ensure they are carried through to completion.

My colleague, Joe Gallagher, applied Lean principles to the error resolution process in an award-winning problem management improvement project. His team analysed their process to identify value and find waste. As you might expect, they found that the backlog of problems waiting for resolution was one of the waste categories (equal to inventory, one of the six categories of waste identified in Lean).

The problem management team went to work to eliminate this 'inventory'. The result was surprisingly effective. Once the number of outstanding problems was trending downwards, the number of new incidents raised started to decline as well. The figures were so closely correlated that it is hard not to acknowledge that it was the implementation of problem fixes that was having the effect.

Make error resolution a priority to ensure the effectiveness of the problem management process.

You might find that the question 'who raises the change?' will arise. This is usually asked because the problem management process flow in the *ITIL Service Operation* book (Cabinet Office, 2011, p.102) shows a connection to the change management process and, from that, people assume that the problem manager should raise the change. In reality, the responsible SMEs perform the activities related to the implementation of the solution, including raising the request for change. The problem manager will usually lack the knowledge and expertise to formulate the change request in any case.

Before a problem can be closed, the implemented solution must be verified to confirm that the risk of recurrence has been eliminated. A good way to confirm that the problem is no longer causing incidents is to remove any workarounds that were put in place to mitigate the risk, to see if the incidents come back. This might require waiting for a specific event, such as a particular customer transaction, or even for the end of year processing to run. You should know how you are going to test the solution before it is approved for implementation.

15 CLOSING PROBLEMS

REVIEW

Table 15.1 Review states and metrics

Incoming state	Ready for review
Incoming sub-states	Root cause not found, Solution not found, Solution not approved, Resolved, Duplicate, Rejected
Who is involved	PAB, IT management, customers
Outgoing state	Root cause analysis, Error resolution, Deferred, Ready for closure
Outgoing sub-states	(Deferred:) Root cause not found, Solution not found, Solution not approved, Resources pending, Funding pending, Disinvest, Upgrade pending, (Ready for closure:) Resolved, Duplicate, Rejected
Time stamps	Set to Ready for review, set to next agreed state as appropriate
Relevant metrics	Days awaiting review
Calculations	Next time stamp minus Set to Ready for review time stamp

The review stage is a major decision point in the problem management process. It is not explicitly part of the ITIL® process, though it is implied in the closure stage. The problem manager reviews the problem with the relevant stakeholders to agree whether it is ready for closure. The PAB is an appropriate forum to make these decisions.

If a problem is not fully resolved, the risk that it represents remains in the environment and could have further impact in the future. There are three courses of action available.

- If the root cause has not been found, it can be referred back to the investigation stage to see if further analysis might find the cause.

- If the cause is known, but a satisfactory resolution has not been found or was not acceptable, stakeholders can ask for further investigation to find a solution, a better solution or more cost-effective one. The problem goes back into the error resolution stage.

- If neither of these courses of action seems appropriate, you must decide what to do with a problem with an unknown cause or with a cause that cannot or will not be fixed. This is not common, but there needs to be a way to handle problems in this situation when they occur.

There is a tendency to want to close problems. Solving problems is intended to improve stability and reduce the risk of service interruptions. Problems are closed when the cause is fixed, implying that the risk has been identified and eliminated. This is not the case here. In addition, if the problem is not fixed, closing it breaks a fundamental rule of problem management. If it happens again, you have caused yourself to fail one of your most important KPIs: that there should be no recurrent problems (see Chapter 7).

If a problem is not fixed, do not close it.

If there is pressure to close problems when not resolved, focus on the risk management aspect to argue against doing so. The drive to 'close things' is very strong and I have encountered it many times, even in discussion with quite sophisticated and knowledgeable companies. Problem management is all about reducing operational risk, by removing problems that impact negatively on stability. Highlight the risk to stability that an unresolved problem represents to explain better why unsolved problems should be kept open and visible, not closed and hidden away.

THE DEFERRED STATE

Table 15.2 Deferred states and metrics

Incoming state	Ready for review
Incoming sub-states	Root cause not found, Solution not found, Solution not approved, Resources pending, Funding pending, Disinvest, Upgrade pending
Who is involved	PAB, IT management, customers
Outgoing state	Root cause analysis, Error resolution, Ready for closure
Outgoing sub-states	(Ready for closure:) Resolved
Time stamps	Set to Deferred, Follow-up date, Set to next agreed state as appropriate
Relevant metrics	Days in Deferred
Calculations	Next time stamp minus set to Deferred time stamp

A deferred state should be introduced as a pragmatic way to solving the situation when a problem cannot be closed. The *ITIL Service Operation* book makes an oblique reference to this approach (Cabinet Office, 2011, p.105).

A problem can be deferred for a number of reasons, including the following:

- The cause cannot be found and it is necessary to wait for the incident to happen again so that you can get more information (hopefully this should be rare).
- The cause is known but there is no reasonable fix.
- There is a fix but it will not be applied, because:
  - it is too costly financially;
  - budget is not available;
  - it is more expensive than the business impact of the incidents it causes; or
  - appropriate resources are not available.
- The application or infrastructure platform is scheduled for a future upgrade or replacement, which will eliminate the cause.
- The platform or process is to be retired, which means it is not worth fixing the problem.
- The organisation is exiting this business in the near future.

Pending upgrades or retirements are common reasons given. They need to be tracked carefully because upgrade and replacement projects are often delayed and legacy systems and processes have a habit of hanging around for a very long time.

A problem that has been resolved, but is waiting for confirmation, should probably be left in resolution and not deferred unless there is a long delay, such as waiting for an annual event to occur (see Chapter 14).

The key point is that problems should only be deferred by agreement with stakeholders. Again, the PAB is a good forum to govern deferral. To maintain visibility, all deferred state problems should be included in management reporting. This is especially important in situations where the business or customer will not pay for the fix. It helps people remember that the problem is not fixed, that it was deferred by agreement for the stated reasons and that they have agreed to bear the risk. This can facilitate a conversation around whether it is now time to revisit that decision, address the uncertainty or inconvenience and invest in a solution to address the problem, or reconfirm that they are content to continue to live with the risk.

The key to using the deferred state is to revisit deferred problems regularly and to maintain visibility through reporting problems. That way, management and customers can be satisfied that risks are being managed appropriately.

A common concern is that problems could build up in the deferred state and the list will get longer and longer. However, with regular review and effective decision-making, they should not build up. Deferment is still better than closing problems that are not fixed, leaving risks hidden. In addition, if deferred problems do build up, it is an indicator that there is something wrong in the process or its governance. For example, root cause analysis or solution development might be poor, applications and infrastructure might lack essential data gathering instrumentation, there might be a reluctance to fix things or a general state of inertia in the organisation. Problem managers should investigate these factors if deferred problems increase.

Keep track of problems in the deferred state by setting follow-up dates, perhaps by using a due date function, if your system includes it. Run reports to list problems that are due for review either by the problem manager or by bringing them to the PAB. Problems that are overdue for review is a good metric to track (see Chapter 7).

CLOSURE

Table 15.3 Closure states and metrics

Incoming state	Ready for closure
Incoming sub-states	Resolved, Duplicate, Rejected
Who is involved	PAB, IT management, customers
Outgoing state	Closed
Outgoing sub-states	Resolved, Duplicate, Rejected
Time stamps	Date and time closed
Relevant metrics	Total days open
Calculations	Closed time stamp minus Opened time stamp

Problems should only be closed with approval and after confirmation that the problem is fixed. The PAB is probably the best forum to give approval, at least for major problems. Certainly, individual problem managers or other stakeholders should not be able to close problems without some sort of independent review.

The main assessment criterion is the strength of the testing that was done. While you can often be quite sure a problem is fixed, you might only be able to get proof 'beyond reasonable doubt'. Criteria for closure need to be clearly stated to allow a good decision.

All closed problems should be reported as part of the formal communications process, but also to celebrate success and acknowledge the investigating and resolving teams.

Maintain a register of closed problems to 'keep score' and to remind management of the effectiveness of the process.

Perform quality checks as well. All records should be fully up to date and, so that information is available for future use, all related knowledge articles and known errors should be reviewed for accuracy and completeness.

Do you ever reopen a closed problem? I tend to open a new problem record if it is felt that a problem has recurred and link it to the previous one. The new problem will contain a task to investigate what went wrong with the previous investigation. Alternatively, you could flag the old one as closed in error. Whether you reopen or not, there will be issues with statistics and reporting, but I think opening a new problem is simpler and less confusing. Which approach you take will probably have some tool dependencies to consider as well.

MAJOR PROBLEM REVIEW

Major problem reviews (MPRs), like major incident reviews, are an extension of the post-implementation review, which is recommended as the final step in most project methodologies to close the project. While there are circumstances where it might be appropriate to perform an MPR, for example if there were issues raised with how the problem was run or if it took a long time to find the cause, I think it is unnecessary to make it a permanent feature of the problem process and run one for every major problem.

Many of the advantages proposed for this review, such as identifying actions to prevent recurrence and third-party follow-ups, or opportunities for proactive problem management (Cabinet Office, 2011, p.105), should already have happened during the problem investigation. Certainly customer awareness of actions taken to prevent recurrence should happen throughout the course of the investigation and particularly as part of closure.

Only run MPRs when required. It should be obvious from the progress of an investigation when it is appropriate to perform one.

CONCLUSION

I think that implementing effective problem management is one of the most beneficial steps that you can take to improve your IT services. It is not hard to get right, even though many people will tell you it is difficult to implement. The more problem management I do, the more I find that it is the organisational change factors that cause the most difficulty. It takes time and understanding to bring people around to the new way of thinking. Along the way, they need to be shown that problem management is not a threat, it is not aimed at 'finding the culprits' or exposing people's failings. Be patient and recognise that you cannot change people, they can only change themselves. Make 'assign no blame' your mantra and emphasise the structured approach.

I hope this book has been of some use to you as you introduce, improve or re-invigorate problem management in your organisation. I wish you every success.

ONLINE RESOURCES

The following additional resources can be downloaded from www.bcs.org/probmgt-extras

SAMPLE BUSINESS CASES

Detailed business case

Brief business case

SAMPLE IMPLEMENTATION PLAN

SAMPLE LAUNCH AND FAMILIARISATION TRAINING

ROOT CAUSE CODES

FURTHER READING

Agile Admin, The (2011) *What is DevOps?* http://theagileadmin.com/what-is-devops/. Accessed 29 April 2014.
   A very straightforward introduction to this topic, with quite a few references for further exploration.

Ammerman, M. (1998) *The root cause analysis handbook*. Boca Raton, USA: CRC Press.
Andersen, B. and Fagerhaug, T. (2006) *Root cause analysis: simplified tools and techniques*. Milwaukee, USA: Quality Press.
Okes, D. (2009) *Root cause analysis: the core of problem-solving and corrective action*. Milwaukee, USA: Quality Press.
   Three books from the quality movement. Each gives a different view of problem management from a non-IT perspective. I like the Okes book best, but Ammerman contains good information about causal factor analysis and control barriers. Interesting reading for problem managers.

Brooks, P. (2006) *Metrics for IT service management*. Zaltbommel, NL: Van Haren Publishing.

Cabinet Office (2007) *ITIL service operation (v3)*. London: TSO.
Cabinet Office (2011) *ITIL service operation (2011 edition)*. London: TSO.
   The 2011 edition is, of course, only a guide, because it does not have the space to go into a thorough discussion of all aspects. Having said that, it is a very good guide and well worth reading as a starting point for thinking about problem management.

Chandoo (2009) *Pareto charts: how to do Pareto analysis using Excel*. http://chandoo.org/wp/2009/09/02/pareto-charts/. Accessed October 2014.
   Very clear instructions on how to do it, plus a downloadable template. A great general how-to site for Excel® as well.

Gawade, A. (2011) *The checklist manifesto: how to get things right*. London: Profile Books.
   A great book that sets out an elegant and simple approach to process improvement and problem prevention. It applies lessons from the airline industry to apply the checklist approach to improving outcomes in operating theatres (Gawade is a surgeon). It has application to any process or endeavour, not just the medical field.

George, M.L., Rowlands, D. and Kastle, B. (2004) *What is Lean Six Sigma?* New York: McGraw-Hill.
> A short handbook that gives an excellent overview of what Lean Six Sigma is, what it does and how to apply it.

George, M.L., Rowlands, D., Price, M. and Maxey, J. (2005) *The Lean Six Sigma pocket toolbook*. New York: McGraw-Hill.
> This book is full of valuable explanations of how many common cause identification and verification tools work, as well as statistics, data gathering, control charts, process evaluation and general analysis approaches. I find it a very useful reference because every topic is only a couple of pages long and it gets to the point very quickly, with lots of diagrams and illustrations.

Gilbert, A. and Hutchinson, J. (2009) *How to save time and money by managing organisational change effectively*. Bodmin and King's Lynn, UK: MPG Books Group.
> This book pulls together a lot of well-researched and established knowledge about organisational change in just a few short pages (under 70). With so much of problem management either impacting or impacted by organisations, knowledge of these topics is pretty much mandatory for all problem managers.

Haughey, D. (no date) *Pareto analysis step by step*. http://www.projectsmart.co.uk/pareto-analysis-step-by-step.html. Accessed October 2014.
> A short and simple explanation of the principle from the project management world. Easy to understand and practical. This is a good general project management resource website as well.

Lewis, J.P. (2007) *Fundamentals of project management (3rd edition)*. New York: AMACOM.
> This is one of the classic short texts on project management. Problem managers (indeed, professionals in many disciplines) should have at least a basic understanding of project management and this book is a good place to start. This is especially important in the error resolution phase of managing problems.

O'Loughlin, E.F.M. (2009) *Problem-solving techniques #1: Pareto analysis*. http://www.youtube.com/watch?v=dENYL2mk4OE. Accessed October 2014.
> For those who like things explained visually. A lecturer at the National College of Ireland, O'Loughlin has a whole series on problem-solving, everything from Ishikawa to value analysis.

Pascale, R., Sternin, J. and Sternin, M. (2010) *The power of positive deviance*. Boston, USA: Harvard Business Press.
> The subtitle of this book is 'How unlikely innovators solve the world's toughest problems' and it is not wrong. This book is about very complex problems in social contexts – child malnutrition in Vietnam, infection control in major hospitals, infant mortality. A very large step beyond the problems we face in IT. However, the unique approach is very powerful and something we, as practitioners, can learn from, particularly when problems are very difficult.

Rudd, C. (2010) *ITIL v3 planning to implement service management*. London: TSO.

Smith, R. and Hutchinson, J. (2011) *How to make a difference by transforming managers into leaders*. Woodhouse Eaves, UK: Go MAD Press.

Standards Australia (2004) *Risk management guidelines (Companion to AS/NZS 4360:2004, Handbook HB 436:2004)*. Sydney, Australia: Standards Australia; Wellington, NZ: Standards New Zealand.

Wheeler, D.J. (2003) *Making sense of data: SPC for the service sector*. Knoxville, USA: SPC Press.
    This book makes the statistical analysis of process data easy to understand (well, as easy as it is ever going to get, anyway). A 'must have' for anyone serious about process improvement. With chapter titles like 'Do people really do this stuff?' and 'What are you trying to do?', it is absolutely rooted in the real world.

REFERENCES

Anderson, S. (2009) Root cause analysis: addressing some limitations of the five whys. *Quality Digest.* http://www.qualitydigest.com/inside/fda-compliance-news/root-cause-analysis-addressing-some-limitations-5-whys.html. Accessed October 2014.

Buzan, T. (2104) *Think Buzan: the inventors of Mind mapping.* http://thinkbuzan.com/. Accessed 31 May 2014.

Cabinet Office (2011) *ITIL service operation (2011 edition).* London: TSO.

Carter, M. (2012) *The 8-disciplines problem-solving methodology.* Brea, USA: 6ixsigma. org Inc. (Kindle edition).

CMMI Institute (2014) *CMMI appraisals.* http://cmmiinstitute.com/cmmi-solutions/cmmi-appraisals/. Accessed 31 May 2014.

Dekker, S. (2006) *The field guide to understanding human error.* Farnham, UK: Ashgate Publishing.

Dennis Adams Associates Limited. http://www.dennisadams.co.uk/. Accessed October 2014.

Dörner, D. (1996) *The logic of failure.* Cambridge, USA: Basic Books.

Dugmore, J. and Lacy, S. (2011) *A manager's guide to service management (6th edition).* London: British Standards Institution.

England, R. (2011) *Basic service management.* Porirua, New Zealand: Two Hills Ltd.

Falkowitz, R. (2011) *IT tools for the business when the business is IT.* London: TSO.

Gallagher, J. (2012) *How does enterprise level problem management categorise problems (how deep do you dive into the RCA)?* ITIL® Problem Management Forum, LinkedIn, http://www.linkedin.com/groups?home=&gid=1020547. Accessed October 2014.

George, M.L., Rowlands, D., Price, M. and Maxey, J. (2005) *The Lean Six Sigma pocket toolbook.* New York, USA: McGraw-Hill.

Gilbert, A. and Hutchinson, J. (2009) *How to save time and money by managing organisational change effectively.* Bodmin and King's Lynn, UK: MPG Books Group.

Gilbert, A. and Smith, R. (2008) *How to save time and money by managing meetings effectively.* Woodhouse Eaves, UK: Go MAD Books.

Gilkey, C. (2012) *The difference between critical success factors and key performance indicators.* http://www.productiveflourishing.com/the-difference-between-critical-success-factors-and-key-performance-indicators/. Accessed October 2014.

Hagel, J., Brown, J.H. and Davidson, L. (2009) The big shift: measuring the forces of change. *Harvard Business Review,* 87 (7/8). pp.86–89.

Harrin, E. (2007) *Shortcuts to success: project management in the real world.* Swindon: BCS, The Chartered Institute for IT.

Hong, L. and Page, S.E. (2004) Groups of diverse problem solvers can outperform groups of high-ability problem solvers. *Proceedings of the National Academy of Sciences of the United States of America.* 101 (46), pp.16,385–16,389. http://www.pnas.org/content/101/46/16385.full. Accessed 27 April 2014.

ISACA (2013) *COBIT® self-assessment guide: using COBIT 5* http://www.isaca.org/COBIT/Pages/Self-Assessment-Guide.aspx. Accessed October 2014.

Jones, D. (2012) The argumentative ape. *New Scientist,* 26 May 2012. p.35.

Joosten, M. (2011) *The added value of a facilitator when troubleshooting as a group.* KT http://www.kepner-tregoe.com/pdfs/articles/Facilitation110426.pdf. Accessed October 2014.

Kahnemann, D. (2012) *Thinking, fast and slow.* London: Penguin Books.

Kaplan, R.S. and Norton, D.P. (1996) *The balanced scorecard.* Boston, USA: Harvard Business School Press.

Kaplan, R.S. and Norton, D.P. (2001) *The strategy-focused organisation.* Boston, USA: Harvard Business School Press.

Kepner, C.H. and Tregoe, B.B. (2006) *The new rational manager: an updated edition for a new world.* Princeton, USA: Princeton Research Press.

Kepner–Tregoe (2010) *KT ITSM problem and incident management.* July 2011 course notes and reference.

Kepner–Tregoe (2014) http://www.kepner-tregoe.com/. Accessed 29 May 2014.

King, Z. (2012) Genius networks: link to a more creative social circle. *New Scientist,* 2866, 29 May 2012. pp.37–39.

Kotter, J.P. (2012) *Leading change.* Boston, USA: Harvard Business Review Press.

Machiavelli, N. (1513) *The prince (Oxford's World Classics edition, 2005).* Oxford: OUP.

Martinez, H. (2009) *How much does downtime really cost?* http://www.information-management.com/infodirect/2009_133/downtime_cost-10015855-1.html?zkPrintable=1&nopagination=1. Accessed October 2014.

McDermott, R.E., Mikulak, R.J. and Beauregard, M.R. (2009) *The basics of FMEA (2nd edition)*. New York, USA: Productivity Press.

Meeting for Results (2013) *Running effective meetings by the book.* http://www.meetingforresults.com/2013/05/29/running-effective-meetings-by-the-book/. Accessed 26 April 2014.

Mind Tools *Brainstorming.* http://www.mindtools.com/brainstm.html. Accessed 29 May 2014.

Mind Tools *Impact probability worksheet.* http://www.mindtools.com/pages/article/worksheets/ImpactProbabilityWorksheet.pdf. Accessed 22 May 2014.

Mind Tools *Mind maps.* http://www.mindtools.com/pages/article/newISS_01.htm. Accessed 29 May 2014.

Mind Tools *8D problem-solving process.* http://www.mindtools.com/pages/article/8d-problem-solving.htm. Accessed 29 May 2014.

NASA (2003) Root cause analysis overview. http://www.hq.nasa.gov/office/codeq/rca/rootcauseppt.pdf. Accessed October 2014.

Offord, P. (2011) *Rapid problem resolution: a problem diagnosis method for IT professionals.* Essex: Advance Seven Limited.

Paradies, M. and Unger, L. (2008) *TapRooT®: changing the way the world solves problems.* Knoxville, USA: System Improvements.

Pascale, R., Sternin, J. and Sternin, M. (2010) *The power of positive deviance.* Boston, USA: Harvard Business Press.

Patterson, H. (2012) *Putting the pieces together: service integration and management for multisourced environments.* http://www.apmdigest.com/putting-the-pieces-together-service-integration-and-management-for-multisourced-environments. Accessed October 2014.

Perlen, M. (2011) *Cost and scope of unplanned outages: winds of change blog.* http://www.evolven.com/blog/costs-and-scope-of-unplanned-outages.html?goback=%2Egmr_686 77%2Egde_68677_member_131722815. Accessed October 2014.

Pink Elephant. *PinkVERIFY.* http://www.pinkelephant.com/pinkverify/. Accessed October 2014.

Poppleton, A. and Holmes, K. (2011) *IT service management for small IT teams.* London: BSI.

Skwire, D. (2009) *First fault software problem-solving*. RoI: Open Task.

TapRooT (2014) *About TapRooT*. http://www.taproot.com/products-services/about-taproot. Accessed 29 May 2014.

Thomas, P., Paul, D. and Cadle, J. (2012) *The human touch – personal skills for professional success*. Swindon, UK: BCS, The Chartered Institute for IT.

Wheeler, D.J. (2003) *Making sense of data: SPC for the service sector*. Knoxville, USA: SPC Press.

Wikipedia *Critical success factors*. http://en.wikipedia.org/wiki/Critical_success_factor. Accessed October 2014.

Womack, J.P. and Jones, D.T. (2003) *Lean thinking: banish waste and create wealth in your corporation*. New York, USA: Free Press.

Workplace Psychology (2012). *The 5 whys (and some limitations)*. http://workplacepsychology.net/2012/02/07/the-5-whys-and-some-limitations/. Accessed October 2014.

Yammer https://www.yammer.com/. Accessed October 2014.

INDEX